HOW MANY MILES TO BABYLON?

Thoughts From A Long Time Writer And Editor

Dorothy Davies

HOW MANY MILES TO BABYLON?

Thoughts From A Long Time Writer And Editor

A FICTION4ALL PAPERBACK

© Copyright 2020
Dorothy Davies

The right of Dorothy Davies to be identified as author and channel of this work has been asserted by him in accordance with the Copyright, Designs and Patents Act 1988.

All Rights Reserved

No reproduction, copy or transmission of the publication may be made without written permission.

No paragraph of this publication may be reproduced, copied or transmitted save with the written permission of the publisher, or in accordance with the provisions of the Copyright Act 1956 (as amended).

Any person who does any unauthorised act in relation to this publication may be liable to criminal prosecution and civil claims for damages.

ISBN: 978-1-78695-259-2

Fiction4All
www.fiction4all.com

This Edition
Published 2020

Dedicated to the memory of Ray Bradbury
August 22, 1920 – June 5, 2012

In recognition of the fact it was his stories which led me into serious writing, acknowledging the pleasure he brought me over so many years and the fact he shared his expertise and knowledge willingly with so many others. This is a small token of the debt I owe him.

Once read, never forgotten.

Your life's work may be done, Ray, but the legacy lives on. If we could all say that, the world would be a better place.

How many miles to Babylon?

Three score miles and ten

Can we get there by candlelight

Yes and back again.

Babylon, here we come!

Part One

From a writer's viewpoint

'I want to be a writer.' Words that come easy for a life that isn't. Writing can be all consuming, all demanding, taking time away from normal interests, sport, TV, visiting, you name it, writing can interrupt it. Memories of making sandwiches from bread I baked the day before, packing a lunch to go on a day trip by coach... the act of making the sandwiches from home-made bread triggered a short story idea. I wrote it in my head all day... no notebook, left home in too much of a hurry, clutching the sandwiches, to think about it... Writing can get between you and work, if you're not careful. The characters tend to ease their way into your thoughts, to demand your attention, to stand on the sidelines waving madly, sometimes with huge flags which say TAKE NOTICE OF US!

If you're already experiencing that, my sympathies. There's no way out, I'm afraid. You're hooked for life.

Equally, welcome to the writing world. It's a demanding profession/way of life but one that writers, on the whole, would not change for anything. The joy of translating an idea into a story or novel, of bringing people alive and letting them walk and talk their way through your pages, cannot be compared to any other way of life. Artists may think they have it pinned down with their easels, palates and paints, but a canvas is not a hefty tome of 100,000 words, is it? So let the painters gather on the hillside to capture the landscape, the sunset, the bowl of fruit and we, the writers, will gather in solitude behind our monitors and let our creations become our companions.

This handbook is a small effort to try and help you on the way of making the idea become a profitable hobby or even a profitable life.

So, what are you waiting for?

Make haste, Babylon is calling...

In the Beginning

The first thing, always, to say to a wannabe writer is: it isn't easy. It looks it, just throwing the words at the screen; see how they fall, arrange them into something resembling paragraphs, send it off and make a fortune.

Come with me; let's see where we can go with this. If I repeat myself, it's in an effort to ensure the message gets through. There are a lot of highly talented writers out there who are failing at the first fence through simple lack of application to the craft and/or a huge ego that says, 'I'm right, you're wrong and if I want to litter my work with OTT language and sex scenes, I will - see you at the Awards Ceremony.' Somehow I don't think so…

***

Writing is a craft that has to be learned.

This book is meant to show you the pitfalls and help you make your MS acceptable to the first real reader you have, outside of your beta readers, that is. (You can discount family who should never be allowed to read your work until it is in print. Because… they all say it's wonderful when it often isn't and you get inflated ideas of how good it is and become bitterly disappointed when the editor sends it back only part read. It happens…)

This advice is given by someone who has been writing all her life, been paid for it for the last 35 years and counting and who has been editing professionally for 20+ years.

I have a whole stack of anthologies to my name and you should be aware that one of them, Comes the Night, was selected for Best Horror 4 by Ellen Datlow. It doesn't come better than that. I knew what I was looking for when it came to quality work to put into any anthology I edited. I made up my mind that Thirteen Press titles were to be the best and worked at getting the standards to the point when sales were guaranteed by the sheer quality of YOUR work. You benefited from that as well as Thirteen Press and Horrified Press who hold the imprint.

I'm not the sweet and sugary type, not going to tell people that with a few stories accepted they're on their way to the big time, but equally I'm not the kind of editor who normally sends stories back without saying why. This upsets some people but that's their ego getting in the way. They're in the group who think they have nothing to learn when in fact all writers are learning all the time.

I'm asking you to accept this book as me trying to push you in the right direction to have acceptances instead of rejections, to feel good about the writing, to know you can make it.

If that's all right with you, let's get into the whole business of writing, shall we?

***

So… what's the secret of success and how do you go about getting there?

The first thing is... accepting that writing is an apprenticeship that never ends. We all learn all the time, how to craft the story, create the characters, make every word count, write to tight word limits (stories and articles) find catchy/interesting/attention-grabbing titles, conjure scenarios that are believable (no logic slip-ups) have a story which holds the reader's attention from beginning to end and all this done in a writing style that is entirely your own.

The second thing is... none of this comes in a hurry. No artist ever created a masterpiece first time they picked up a brush, no composer wrote a symphony first time out. It's practice and more practice. My first efforts at writing were rejected. I tried writing something for a correspondence course and had it torn to pieces. I almost gave up but something made me keep right on writing. Slowly but surely the rejections changed to acceptances; a good many of my stories appeared in fanzines, unpaid, a limited audience but acceptances for all that. It made the difference; it was the impetus I needed to keep on writing. When I began it was all typed, I worked on a Brother portable on the kitchen table for ages. When I wore that out, I bought an Adler, a solid piece of equipment that would withstand a bomb blast, I'm sure it would and on that I wrote my first to-be-published YA novel.

It took eleven years for it to find a publisher. I'm telling you this is to emphasise that none of this comes in a hurry. After eleven years, umpteen retypes and a lot of abortive submissions to agents and publishers, an agent placed the book with Bodley Head. It was published - it sank like a stone.

We're going back before the age of the Internet so there was no marketing I could do. Bodley Head didn't allocate money for publicity, advertisements and the like, so the poor little book slid into oblivion after all my efforts and all my years of trying.

Bodley Head, though, said they were happy with it and did I have another book? I did. I outlined it, another YA book, starting in 495 AD and ending in 1995 AD, every chapter separate, every one linked to the one before and the one after, the theme, First Love. They said it couldn't be done. So I did it. It was accepted, a development fee was paid for me to alter this and revise that, which I did. And it was dropped.

Now comes something you need to think about when you're writing. A book is never finished. I sent that novel to a critique agency and got back pages of advice on how to make it better.

A book was accepted by one of the Big Names in the business and a critique company found goodness knows how many ways I could make it better. They were right, in every way they were right. They saw things a critical editor should have seen but didn't. The revised book 'Forever' is online. Details at the end of this book if you're interested…

The third thing is… you must never stop thinking writing. When you're reading, dissect the story, the grammar, the metaphors; the dialogue tags, ask yourself why the story is holding your attention, why haven't you dropped the book in at the nearest charity shop or book exchange or deleted it from your Kindle or whatever? What's making you read on? Criticise the story in your head; is it draggy here and there, could it have been paced better? (The 'story arc' theory comes in here.) Could the characters have been better delineated? Was the balance of narrative and dialogue about right? These days, when I write, I hear my daughter saying 'don't give me the description; I don't care what colour dress she's wearing, give me the story!' This is valid in many instances; some writers do tend to rely overmuch on background and description. So, think writing. Observe people. How do they walk, how do they talk to one another, using their hands, or flicking their hair or playing with buttons, jewellery, keys, whatever? Be a people watcher. Listen to conversations, note how people speak to one another. Is the dialogue that natural in the book you're reading/writing? People don't speak formally to one another unless they're perfect strangers and even then they're likely to lapse into the occasional 'haven't' rather than 'have not.' Formality is the death of many a story.

If you google Ray Bradbury, the greatest influence when I began writing and surely one of the finest horror/SF/fantasy writers of our time, you will find his lecture to young authors. It's full of worthwhile advice. That link, along with others that might be of help to you, is at the end of this book.

Among the points he makes he says, read a short story every day and a poem every day. The reading is the important part. You need to read short stories to write short stories. It's an art form in itself. Creating an entire scenario, background, characters and storyline in the limited space given by a short story is something you need to read to understand and then try for yourself.

If you can write good short stories, then you're on your way to writing good novels. The one always leads to the other, says me anyway. It's just that you get more space with a novel to expand your background, characters and storyline…

The poem helps you to think poetically. Sometimes metaphors can be a bit dull, reading poetry for its rhythm and sense can help you find the right words you need. I read John Drinkwater poems all the time, it's where I find my titles (more on titles later) and where I lose myself in the wonderful rhythmic patterns he creates. I was also fortunate enough to have a poem sent to me every day by Ken L Jones, poet, writer and friend.

Now go find your stories and poems…

Storytelling

A radio programme on second-hand bookshops included the presenter discussing with a book shop owner the fact that people still came in to buy books by the old authors; Warwick Deeping was one he named. (I love his books.) "They want the old storytellers," he said and they do. Catherine Cookson, for example, sold millions, even though to all intents and purposes she was telling the same old story over and over. Because - each time it came out new and fresh. She was a story-teller, first and foremost.

I recently re-acquired a book I knew and loved in my teens. The question was; would it stand up to today's cynical reading? It turned out to be as compelling a read now as when I read it before. It bears out my theory. Agnes Sligh Turnbull has the ability (still) to make me turn the page, even though I knew what was to come.

My other favourite read-over-and-over-again authors are Howard Spring, who can evoke both Cornwall and characters in a way no one else has ever been able to do - for me, Nevil Shute who can get even non-technical me involved in aircraft, design and the flying thereof because of the stories he weaves around the facts; R F Delderfield whose large, complex books are crammed with characters which come alive even now, many years after his death, and every book by Ray Bradbury. When I tire of modern writers with their sharp sentences and glitzy settings, I go back to the old storytellers, the ones who could take their time and spin out a description and can still - even after many readings - make me weep over a death.

And yes, I have read every Warwick Deeping I could find.

Also on my 'read countless times' shelves are RD Blackmore's Lorna Doone, Jerome K Jerome's Three Men In A Boat, H de Vere Stacpoole's The Blue Lagoon, Peter S Beagle's A Fine And Private Place and the entire works of Charles Dickens. Then there is the whole of Stephen King's The Dark Tower series, plus The Stand and 11.22.63. He too is a master storyteller. The remainder of his books are in my Kindle.

Any books on writing will tell you how to write, (sort of, everyone has different ideas) how to set out a manuscript and how to present it properly for your publisher. Articles will tell you about grammar and characterisation, viewpoint and using flashback. These are all essential, but they can't tell you the one thing you need more than anything else - a story.

Before anything else then, consider your plotline. Does it demand the reader turn the pages to find out what is going to happen next? Is your background so vivid it leaps from the page - paints pictures for your reader? Did the story move you when you wrote it, or was it a cold clinical exercise of words on paper? If that's the case, it's likely they won't move your reader, either. While it's true that the reader can't tell the difference between a page laboured over and one written swiftly, they can tell the difference between a piece written with emotion and one without. If you don't care about your characters, why should your reader?

Find yourself a good strong storyline, one which says something to the world. Then care about your characters, care about them deeply and honestly, portray them and their background, to the best of your ability.

And then perhaps the old art of storytelling, one which comes from early campfires and men in caves to today's hi-tech wizardry, will be back in our lives.

Won't that be wonderful?

What I want to do is guide you through some of the maze that is storytelling, so you reach the centre and the prize without calling for help from the maze builders…

The builders of Babylon can't help, this is a journey you have to make on your own but don't worry; I'm here for a while, at least as long as you're reading my book.

Short Stories

How to...

Let's consider short stories first.

Many years ago – and I do mean many – I used to buy a magazine called John O'London's and read it on the train commuting to and from the City of London, where I worked. They ran a competition, as most magazines do.

The prize winning story has never left me. I cannot remember the author or the title but the storyline...

A young boy is waiting for his father to return home from the war. His mother has told him many times that his father is a hero, he has decorations; he is a great man. The boy looks at pictures of ancient Romans with their laurels and thinks that's how his father's going to look when he comes. He is busy rushing around looking for a gift for this great man, this hero, when he sees his favourite china dog. In his rush to wrap it, he drops it and an ear is broken off. At that moment he hears his mother calling 'Your father's here!" He rushes to the window.... and sees an ordinary man in an ordinary overcoat looking up at him. He steps back, bitterly disappointed. The dream is crushed. The dog with only one ear would do after all.

Simple. Heartbreaking in many ways. I wondered many times if the story came from real life, it had that honest feel. Simply written, simply expressed. That story has stayed with me.

I edited an anthology called In The Darkness. One of the stories which came in had the same effect, it won't leave me. Sadly for me, the author never responded to emails and requests to sign a contract, so I couldn't use it. It makes no difference in some ways, I've read the story; I won't forget it. I just wish I could have shared it with the world.

Ray Bradbury's short stories live with me. The October Country is one of the finest collections of brooding poetic horror stories I have read. I know them all and love them all.

Will you write stories that live in people's minds? It should be your aim, for no one wants to expend all that time, energy and inspiration on something that is immediately forgotten once the eyes have travelled over the page.

There's a whole section coming up on creating vivid realistic characters, you'll need to learn to do this to make your story outstanding - but they need a good story to live in. So, because some people find it hard to garner ideas, I've added an appendix of 75 story ideas as a small gift. Really, though, the best stories are the ones you find by watching, thinking, watching and dreaming. The main question always is 'what if', that's the one that leads you into the by-ways of a story.

Short stories are a snapshot of life; a novel is the whole life. That's a fairly simple way of describing the difference. Short stories can start at 6 words:-

For sale. Baby shoes. Not worn.

And end up at 25,000 where they are classed as novellas and are difficult to place. The average story is around 2000-2500 (for me, anyway) but they can go to 5000 without pushing the limits too much. Within that word limit you need to create background and characters with realistic storyline and dialogue. Not an easy task but if you can successfully write short stories, the novel comes a little easier. Not much but a little.

The first real advice is read short stories. As many as you can. Read the anthologies Horrified Press is putting out for its various imprints. Read collections of short stories, see what works for you and what doesn't. If one doesn't work, rationalise why, so you avoid the same pitfall yourself. What happened? Was the story weak, the characters weak or the whole not written vividly enough? Every time you read something you don't like, ask yourself why. I know my hates, you need to find yours.

Read critically, just as I advise you to read novels. What works in this, why does it work, what's the magic that held my attention to the end?

Having conceived a first class story idea, the work begins.

You're sitting there with a head full of ideas and fingers on the keyboard, are you ready to start? It's best, when starting, not to think 'where's this going? How long does it have to be?' and all the other questions you'll ask yourself when you become more experienced. The starting point is The Story. Is it different, entertaining, full of action and drama… well, perhaps not all of that but you get the idea.

The first task is finding the sentence that will grab the reader's attention and draw them in to the story you have to tell. Although the famous Bulwer-Lytton opening line 'It was a dark and stormy night' is now an accepted joke, it actually draws you into the story, if you think about it. What does the storm have to do with anything... who's out in it... who's threatened by it... this is the way you need to think when starting a story. Choosing your opening sentence is important as it sets the scene and theme for the rest of it.

Next, Point of View, first person or third? What feels right to you? Does it matter if your story is limited to what the hero/heroine sees, hears and does and nothing else? Remember that, it's one thing some newbies fall down on, they include information the characters couldn't know because they weren't there. The 'meanwhile back at the ranch' syndrome. Watch out. It can take you unawares.

Having decided which POV to use, you then need to be sure you stick with that person if you can. Switching POV from one character to another in a short story is not a good idea. In a book you can switch because there is plenty of time and space to signal to the reader a change is coming: you either do a two line paragraph break to indicate a change of scene or outright start a new chapter. A short story doesn't allow you to do that. A story that has the hero killed off before the end and the killer or the monster finishing the story is all very well, I have actually accepted a few like that, but it isn't really good and should be done better than that. It can be, with thought.

Point of View is a big subject; there are books and articles on line about it. If stuck, check them out. In any event, studying will help you be a more knowledgeable writer, so it's worth doing.

What you need to remember most of all is that the reader empathises with the first person they 'meet' in a story or a book. If you introduce someone and immediately kill them off (which happens) the reader has to start over again with the next person and by then usually has lost a degree of sympathy with the story – and possibly the writer. Remember the phase horror books went through? The opening chapter/prologue was someone out jogging, running, shopping, whatever, and they are outlined to the reader at length, age, hair colour, name, where they live, what they did for a living and then hey! They're killed off by the murderer/monster/whatever and the book carries on with the real hero, the one who will discover the murderer/kill the monster/whatever. Not good. Wasn't then, isn't now.

So, opening lines. Must attract attention. The attention span of the current population of this earth is shrinking by the day. A discussion has been going on in a writing forum: word count, does it matter. The consensus so far is that shorter is better as people are too impatient to read a big fat book. ??? These are writers! Can't read a big fat book? Looks like War and Peace is dead and gone, then…

Remember the golden rule. EVERYTHING and EVERY WORD in the story must carry that story forward to its LOGICAL conclusion. So, try and avoid starting your story with people sitting around eating unless the eating is a part of the story.

Try and avoid starting with someone getting up, washed, dressed, etc, unless that too is part of the story. If they're going to college, Uni or work, avoid the traffic chaos, busy mall, who they see on the way unless that too is an integral part of the story. I've seen all of this and have deleted paragraphs of it, starting the story where it needs to start, with action. With drama. With attention grabbing words.

I remember critiquing a story where the heroine came home in the rain, opened her front door, put the dripping umbrella in a stand, hung up the wet coat, took off her rubbers, went into the kitchen and put the kettle on for a hot drink... by which time I was bored senseless. Remember that short attention span. See what you can cut and do it. Look for unwanted unnecessary dialogue. There is a section on dialogue in the character part of the book, but before then...

People do not spell everything out as I just did with this sentence.

People don't spell it out. They talk in shorthand. They aren't formal with one another unless of course you're at a Garden Party at Buckingham Palace and the Queen is likely to stroll by. 'Are you going to' usually becomes 'you gonna...'Listen to the way people talk to one another. The original greeting 'good morning' has been reduced to 'morning' (although we have lengthened the goodbye with 'have a nice day' – what if I don't want to, can't, am too ill to have such a thing... but it's 'nice', I suppose.) Try some shorthand with your dialogue, cut the formalities; use contractions. It works. Believe me it does. Only when issuing orders do you need to be formal, so there's no possibility of a mistake. Or very little, anyway.

Be dramatic. Start your story with eye catching dialogue. This is one of my favourite stories about the bodysnatchers in London:

'Shut the damn door, Crouch!'

'What's up, Joseph? Too cold for you? Get too hot in here and the stiffs'll start to rot. That what you want?'

They're in the Fortune of War pub in the City of London, right opposite St Bartholomew's Hospital. (In one year 187 bodies went into Barts... but that's for another time, another place.)

Having got your opening line in place, your next task is to make sure the rest of the story matches up, action, dialogue; narrative, all equally balanced and, even more important, with no unnecessary words.

"She reached out her arm to turn off the light."

"She turned off the light."

A simple example but this is the kind of thing you should be looking for. There is a lot of superfluous writing in the stories being submitted; I take a razor to every one that comes in, deleting that kind of over-writing. Try some flash fiction, limiting yourself to 200-300 words, see how much you can cut out and still keep both storyline and impact. Why not enter the weekly Challenge (details at the end of this book)? Regular 'playing', as in writing a story every week, teaches you the art of sharp writing, full of emotion and back story, holding the attention. Yes, we are back to that again. Without that element, no story or book is worth your time and effort.

The example I came up with of 'she turned out the light' sparked the memory of a story in one of the famous Pan Book of Horror Stories series.

The basis is a young man seducing a woman. They drink, they talk, they go to her bedroom, they kiss; they tumble into bed at which point the young man says: 'oh dearest, we left the light on!' And she reaches out her arm which grows and grows until she can touch the light switch...

So sometimes – just sometimes – that line works!

Another small diversion here, if I may, to prove a point. I'll be diverting from time to time, examples often help clarify what I'm on about.

I misread information on-line and sent a story to an editor for an anthology which had already closed. He said this and then said the title had intrigued him, (The Day Death Wore Boots) so he read the story. It subsequently appeared in the 2013 issue of Science Fiction Trails.

Title. Opening line. Capturing attention. Getting published. I know the opening line worked: if it hadn't, he wouldn't have read the story, no matter how clever the title.

Next is the body of the story, where all the action takes place, balanced throughout as dialogue, narrative and action, bringing it round to the ending, the second most important part. Endings shouldn't trail off; they should be emphatic, final; definite and conclude the story, not leave the reader wondering what it was all about.

None of this happens overnight, or even over a weekend. It takes time, a lot of it and a LOT of writing. You need to explore your abilities, discover what your strengths and weaknesses are, discover which format feels right to you; which genre is really suited to you. Your horror writing might be more fantasy when it comes down to the real heart of it.

No writing is wasted. You could write twenty stories without success and be downhearted, but the germ of the writing is there. The stories can be rewritten and improved later on when you're more experienced. The main thing is, you're writing, you can call yourself a writer. The words are going from the keyboard to the screen, something is being created. Every story helps you take a step nearer to publication, to having the work read by a wider audience than your would-be editor.

Every critique you receive takes you one step nearer, too. If you're fortunate enough to get a critique, study it, think about it, absorb it, make it part of your writing in the future. Has an editor said your characters are not fully formed? It's easy to create cardboard cut-outs, you have to work at fully fledged thinking winking walking talking working people who come off the page and become memorable. That too is something that only comes with time and experience. But you'll get there, if you're determined; if you write enough.

One thing you need to look out for, something that might be commented on if you're fortunate enough to get a critique, is SHOW DON'T TELL.

This is simply expressed but often hard to write in.

Example:

"I hate you!" he shouted angrily.

He thumped the wall, loosening the plaster. "I hate you!"

One tells us that he is angry; the other shows it in a more vivid way. This is what you're looking for, the alternative way of showing what's going on in the story. If you can use dialogue instead of a 'he did this' tag, it will work. The work will begin to come alive.

Watch your tenses. Stories can be in the past or the present, but not both unless you are very skilled. Too many 'has' instead of 'had' creeping in destroys the tenses and causes mayhem with the reader (your editor.)

Watch those hanging sentences which I detest.

Walking into the room, James took off his coat and poured a drink.

Don't tell me you've not seen that in books and longed, seriously longed to red ink it and say, 'rewrite it!' James walked into the room, took off his coat and poured a drink. He can't walk in; take off his coat and pour a drink all at the same time unless he's a mutant or an alien. So, be logical with your characters' actions.

Watch over-use of commas. 99 times out of 100 you do not need one before and; the 'and' itself is enough of a pause. There are times when a list, 'The snarling leaping foaming dog' may seem to be crying out for commas, but is it? Sometimes the running together of a set of words makes a bigger impact. The trick is to read the sentence aloud, pausing at the commas you've put in and see what effect that has on the flow of the words. I experimented with one of my novels. I asked Word to strip every comma out and then went back over it, putting them in where I thought they should go. The book was faster paced, more fluid, for me, much better. (It was published twice; it must have had something going for it…)

Watch placing of commas, it makes a whole world of difference. As in:

Shall we move Henry?

Shall we move, Henry?

Finally in this section, a reminder to study the apostrophe. That seems to be the biggest problem 90% of writers have. The amount of wrongly placed apostrophes is astronomical.

Go study Lynn Truss' 'Eats Shoots and Leaves' book. It gives you everything you need to know about them and a lot more besides. It's funny too, which is always a bonus.

Before you get that far, remember this simple rule:

Invariably it's is IT IS. Read the sentence.

You write: The dog had it's ball.

And it reads: the dog had it is ball.

It's is also IT HAS in some sentences. Same thing, read it aloud. See whether it makes sense.

You use it when something belongs, the dog's ball. If there are more dogs than the single one, the dogs' ball. My brother's bicycle.

You use it for contractions, when you need to unformalise your dialogue which is like thick chunks of plasterboard.

It is a shame we cannot go down that road.

It's a shame we can't go down that road.

It's easy to get it right, but few do.

Correct punctuation goes a long way to your story being read with a degree of interest by the editor.

Another thing to watch for, no; make that two things to watch for. The first is bouncing revolving travelling eyes.

Her eyes went to the door.

His eyes fell on the table.

His eyes went round the room.

We all do it. I commented on it to one thriller writer, who overdid it in one of his books, he said it was a way of writing. Problem is… many years back I saw a cartoon in a fanzine, a man sitting at the table with both eyes dropping and bouncing like rubber balls. It was captioned *his eyes fell on the table*. Once seen, never forgotten. Now that 'eyes' thing hits me every time I see it. I work at excluding it from my stories. How about excluding it from yours?

The other one is the 'magician at work' syndrome. He turned into a side road. He turned into a car park. He turned into the road before his house.

Smart person here, turning himself into just about anything but a human being…

There is an alternative, there always is.

He drove into the side road.

He steered the car into the side road.

He navigated into the side road.

At last, there was the road he needed. One turn of the wheel and he was almost home.

A million ways to get round the magician. Just use your imagination. Do that one thing I've commented on before – think!

Babylon's not in sight yet, there are still many miles to go. You might need a fresh candle.
There's one in the cupboard...

Logic

This has a section of its own for one very big reason: it plays a very big part in your storytelling.
 I decided to put it in here, with the short stories, as that's where I keep seeing the biggest breakdown in logic but this also rolls over into the novels you will doubtless want to write at some time.

First there is the logic of the storyline. Everything, every last thing, has an effect on something else. So... whether it's magic or a fight or a death or an accident, it all has a knock on effect somewhere with someone. Usually a lot of someones.
 Coincidentally, this came up in conversation recently in my shop, when a customer mentioned that if you have a problem with someone, killing them is not the answer, but some people think it's the only way. The conversation then went on to list the knock on effect of a murder, the amount of people it hurts/damages on both sides and everyone that both people knew. Remember, nothing happens in isolation. You hit another car in an accident and two drivers, possibly passengers as well, can be hurt, then there is the problem of not having a car for some time, the after effects of the accident on the drivers, both mental and physical and so it goes on.
 I saw the after effects of an accident one time. The ambulance personnel were working on someone in the bus shelter, the car was blocking the road. The police car was screaming its way to the

scene. So there we have – 5-6 people involved already, maybe more.

Then there was the traffic tailback. It went on and on and on... and any one of them could be late for some very important appointment, a date, a lunch that would be burned, someone who would be angry, thinking they were not wanted, someone could be ill, sick, needing a bathroom urgently... one accident, a hundred or more people affected, before we get into families, hospitals, accident investigators, insurance companies...

Logically, then, you need to think through the reaction to any action anyone takes in your story or novel. The consequences can be quite far reaching. That in itself is the key to a million stories.

The other logic concerns your characters. Two stories came in recently, one featuring a very young boy who appeared to fully understand the concept of democracy as practiced in the USA. Democracy is a huge concept; I doubt very much the average person could adequately describe it in a few words. The fact the child was aware of it in his thoughts seemed entirely wrong.

Another story had a child speaking and thinking like an adult, using adult words and concepts for a horror story. It didn't work.

The secret of making a story work, as I showed with the prize winning one from so far back in my life, is to pitch the thoughts and speech not only to the age but the approximate level of the child's thinking and understanding, too. In Stephen King's IT he has the boys discussing their pre-pubescent idea of what sex is about. It is almost funny until you realise that's the way most boys believed it to be – before the days of Internet and porn, which shows them how it really happens. Remember your own adolescence; your mis-held ideas because you were too embarrassed to ask anyone, remember your simplistic way of thinking and work to capture that with your characters.

Then there is – history. For the distant past, you need to check everything in reputable books (not the easiest thing to find, historians borrow from other historians without checking whether the first one has it right. The 1833 booklet on the great tournament fought by Antony Woodville, KG, Lord Scales of Newcelles and the Isle of Wight, 2nd Earl Rivers, clearly shows…) but it's necessary to at least check dates and places. Shakespeare tossed facts out of the window to make a good story, he got away with it. No internet at that time to catch him out and no clever clogs around either to say he had it wrong. You won't get away with it.

An example. Some years back there was a drama on TV featuring a particular aeroplane. A week or so later a letter appeared in the Radio Times from the pilot of the plane. He had the original log book, showing where it had landed, when it had been serviced, who serviced it… you can't get away with things these days!

Are you writing pre-or post Internet? I read a lot of 'old' writers' work, where all the men seem to smoke pipes, (the cigarettes came later), where everyone wore ties and hats, always the hats, smart suits and overcoats. Now we are much more casual but be aware of the dates when these things changed, when women began wearing trousers, when men stopped wearing ties. When cigarettes were commonplace and no one insisted you stand outside to smoke. When children sat outside pubs to wait for their parents. When holidays were rarities and the occasional day out at the coast was the high point of the year. When people wrote letters which were delivered the same day and urgent news was sent by telegram. Or even good news: a friend has kept a telegram sent by her father over forty years ago, offering congratulations on her first art exhibition.

A different world. A different time. When records were 78 RPM and shattered if you weren't careful with them, when gramophones were wind up, when dances were held every week and you could be sure to meet a future partner there.

This is all under the heading of LOGIC because it has to be logical. If you set a story or novel at any time other than the present, something will have changed. A friend needed a book on the dates when motorways were cut through the countryside as it affected the village where her characters lived.

If you use music as a reference, be sure it was released when you say it was.

Check everything. One of my novels had a sequence set in the late 60s. I was convinced the evening newspapers on sale at street corners included The Star. It didn't.

Films are criticised endlessly for making mistakes, such as Titanic having over 400 errors for paintings out of time, etc. Your story/book will fall down on its little face if there are errors like that. Immediately the reader loses empathy with the whole thing, they put it down and decide never to read anything by that author again. You do not want that!

On that subject, watch with an eagle eye for the other errors. Change of colour of clothing within one scene, sending a character on holiday and bringing them back too soon, giving someone an illness or disability and then forgetting about it later on... this is where those character outlines are immensely useful. If someone needs two keys to get into an apartment, then it has to stay that way, not suddenly change that they get in with one. It trips up the story. It upsets the reader.

Our lives run on logic, make sure your story does, too. Check and remember the ages of your characters, so nothing goes wrong there as the story proceeds. If there's foul weather, make sure it's consistently foul, not suddenly becoming mild for no apparent reason.

Sometimes the temptation to alter a scenario to fit the storyline becomes overwhelming. Don't give in...

Storytelling, beginning, middle and end
But not always necessarily in that order

Although a reasonable assumption is that the story has an ending... the lecture in this section is: don't bore your reader. If you have a slow start, you will lose them. They will flip to the next story in the book but notice your name and possibly avoid buying an anthology with your work in it next time, on the basis why pay for something you're not planning to read? Would you?

A Hollywood screenwriter said, start with action then take 2-3 steps back and bring the story round to that action. It sounds easy but may take a while to be absorbed properly. It makes sense. Start with something that is going to draw the reader's attention, then 'explain' through dialogue and action how that came about. Then wrap the story up with a satisfying ending.

The novel part of this handbook has a lengthy section on characterisation; you might want to take a look. Using that you will find your people coming alive and taking over, which means the beginning, middle and end will be right there, waiting for you to write it.

This will come with experience. That's a given.

But experience means writing, writing and writing. You ready for that?

And finally...

Before we move on to characters and backgrounds and stuff... titles. These need to be interesting, exciting; different. This all means the same thing, doesn't it? Attention grabbing. Sometimes the title comes out of the story/novel itself, sometimes you'll get the title first and write the story around it, sometimes you'll spend hours agonising over finding the right one. I find my titles in the poems of John Drinkwater, just a couple of examples:
>Not The Shadow Of A Man
>Fools and Kings and Fighting Men
>I Diced With God

OK, more than a couple, but I have quite a few books out now and you don't need to know all of them. I just make life more difficult for myself by wanting the poem to match the person. Not The Shadow of a Man is the life of Jacquetta Woodville, who never let her femininity get in the way of her ambitions, Fools and Kings and Fighting Men are the three phases of the life of Charles I.

Is that cheating, I wonder... going to the poetry books? I sometimes read all eleven of them to find the right one, so perhaps not. I also carry a compilation one around with me.

When it comes to stories, the titles come easy for some reason.

For the anthologies I aim for one or two word titles where possible: Arachnophobia, Twisted, Wildwood, Coming Back. Keeping it simple meant there was more room on the cover for the extraordinary artwork Horrified Press came up with for each one. My job was to edit and sort the words which arrived to go between the covers.

Looking for titles, then... listen to people, catch sight of headlines and twist them, or find yourself mis-reading them. Songs are good, I get titles from lyrics, It's a Long Way to Sometime came from a song. Not a title to go on a cover, I admit, but hearing that was the inspiration for a Richard Matheson-type horror flash about a monster. (You need to read it...)

You'll find them everywhere once you become attuned to the need to find the right title for a story, article or novel.

Novels are where we're going next, after the gift I'm leaving for you. This is no more than a small diversion on our journey to Babylon. I think there's yet more candles to be found in the store if you need them

Take a look...

Story ideas

A small gift from me to you – not anywhere near as good as the gifts you'll get when you reach Babylon but it's all right for now. 75 story ideas. Just for you. Follow your thoughts as you read through these, let your imagination run with the concept presented, see how far you can go with a storyline!

1. Revenge is a dish best served cold. After long consideration, how would you deal with a lover who jilted you? The really spectacular ones, disposing of an entire wine cellar, cutting up expensive clothing, ringing the speaking clock in another country and leaving the phone off the hook: boring, all been done. It's time to find some new ones. Here's a few ideas to get you started:
Fill out every coupon for courses, heating, double glazing, whatever you can find, drive them mad with junk mail, but in among the mail comes…?
Drive your lover's car away and post them the keys, leaving them to find it, but when they do…?
Leave notes in conspicuous places if your lover works with you, unsigned and preferably untraceable. Then stand back and watch real things happen!
2. Dear Diary. A young girl is on holiday in Spain and writes in her diary every day. The young waiter sees her and is intrigued. What is the English girl writing? One day she goes off to the pool and leaves her bag behind. He opens it and finds…

3.   A housewife has just received a parcel of goodies when her neighbour comes in, without knocking ... male or female, you decide ... and you decide what goodies are in the parcel.

4.   Days of the week have special significance for a lot of people: Friday, start of the weekend, Monday, start of a new week, new job, new role; new-?

5.   An invitation. A whispered one over a meal, a shouted one across the road, a printed one through the post or dropped through the door. Think about it and the consequences if your hero/heroine attends/does not attend.

6.   What about an invitation which was not intended for you, but you follow through anyway: a letter not meant for you, a parcel not meant for you but which is open and available to be looked at...

7.   Someone loans you a recording of a programme you missed, an instalment of a drama serial, a movie, and when you've done watching, it runs on... (this one is based on real life!)

8.   A recording device has been secretly left running during a conversation...

9.   Foreign holidays: exotic, luxurious, hotels, beaches, beach bars, holiday Romeos, holiday romances, sensual days, steamy nights.

10.   English holidays: guest houses, small and medium priced hotels, great luxurious five crown or five star hotels, with doormen who will get you anything in return for a large folded note. Rainy days on the end of the pier, sunny days in beach huts...

11.   A French car has just driven off the cross Channel ferry, is slowly driving along, trying to get

used to our wonderful clockwise round-the-roundabouts, etc system of roads. The driver stops and picks up a young English hitch hiker…

12. It's _____ 40th birthday. His friends have arranged something a little different for him, not the usual Strip-o-gram.

13. Waitress picks up a note along with the tip, one tended for someone else. Waiter picks up a note along with the tip, one intended for someone else.

14. _____ is a wealthy man; he can buy anything he wants, except _____ who refuses to be bought. What can he do go get her, what can he offer no one else has?

15. After evening classes in French/Spanish/Italian whatever is over, two mature students leave together.

16. A bishop is walking along the road, using a walking stick. Where is he going? Where has he come from?

17. A man in a smart suit with bow tie and briefcase is sitting on the grass verge early in the morning. Why?

18. Keys. What do they open: hotel doors, left luggage compartments, houses, flats, cars, suitcases, writing desks, cabinets, bookcases, shops, files, elevator doors…

19. Metaphorical keys: key words to put someone in a trance, unlock a computer programme, access a file, trigger a command; set a plan in motion…

20. Buying a car. This transaction is fraught with difficulty and possibly a good deal of interaction, whether it's a salesperson, a private

seller or a casual conversation in a pub. All can be twisted to fit a story.

21. Cars: driving, filling them with petrol, using them for love wagons, using them for transport, crashing them, washing them, polishing them, parking them, mending them, garages, motorist shops, greasy mechanics, DIY mechanics, boy racers.

22. Boats: rowing boats, motor boats, river cruisers, river barges, sea going motor boats, yachts, cruise liners, paddle steamers, ferries going somewhere, coming back from somewhere. Working on boats, buying boats, selling boats, sailing boats.

23. Planes: gliders, bi planes, private Lear jets, small private planes, commercial planes. Airports, flying into them, flying out of them. Small private airfields, flying instructors.

24. Trains: fast Intercity trains, commuter trains, Underground trains, steam trains, reclaiming line and rebuilding engines, working on the Underground, working above ground on the main lines, stations, passengers, commuters and holiday makers.

25. Coaches: coach journeys, mystery coach tours, coach holidays, coach drivers, coach stations.

26. Dogs: barking at night, barking during the day, biting someone, threatening someone, fighting to defend their territory, owners tangling in a fight over dogs and then tangling anyway…

27. Cats: sharing two homes, scratching someone, digging up gardens, cat allergies, catching birds

28. Birds: escaped pet ones, feeding wild ones, bird watching, bird studying, exotic birds in homes.

29. Parties: office parties, private parties, cocktail parties, birthday parties, retirement parties. Unwilling spectator to someone else's party in discos, restaurants and the like.

30. Weddings: neglected bridesmaids, maiden aunts, nubile young relatives you've not seen for a while, groom's friends, bride's friends, wild receptions, everything that can go wrong at a wedding.

31. Pubs: upmarket, downmarket, quiet or noisy, secluded or on the main road, travellers who will never come by again, regulars who know everyone...

32. Bookshops: new and second hand, browsers dropping books, finding books, searching for books, leaving messages in books, odd things found in books.

33. Waitresses and waiters overhearing interesting conversations.

34. Jokes: practical jokes often backfire, don't they? Novelty joke items, joke letters which are taken seriously.

35. Valentine cards: receiving or sending can lead to some odd misunderstandings.

36. Neither a borrower or a lender be, but what happens if someone does ask to borrow something and you lend it for a special occasion then can't get it back and you need it for –

37. Neighbourhood watch! Enough said.

38. Breaking a pattern, doing something different, going out a little earlier, a little later, changing a route to work, results in ...

39. Supermarkets: shelf stackers are usually ignored by customers who talk, checkout staff can tell what your lifestyle is by what you buy, what would they say if you changed your buying habits completely?
40. Instead of a supermarket dash, why not a Private Shop dash?
41. Midlife crisis: a theme for many stories of a husband breaking away from the mould to find a younger woman, but does it always have to be like that?
42. Punctuality: would it annoy you, having someone always so precisely on time for everything?
43. Unpunctuality: missing trains, missing appointments, missing deadlines. Many events happen because someone didn't get somewhere he or she said they would.
44. Not turning up at all. What would that mean to a couple waiting on someone's arrival, strangers in a room waiting for an official who never arrived, the witness to a wedding or a signing of some kind.
45. Think about the consequences of leaving a sheet from a book, a letter, a story in a photocopier.
46. Secrets: a world of stories in secrets kept, secrets told, tokens, letters, notes, phone calls, meetings.
47. Mistakes: funny ones, lethal ones, serious ones. Mistakes of identity, place, time, cars, addresses –
48. Letters: love letters, business letters, complaining letters, friendly ones, old ones, delayed ones …

49. Bridges: stone bridges, old bridges, huge iron ones spanning huge rivers, bridges at sunset, bridges at night, bridges as meeting places. Building bridges, burning bridges with people.

50. Neighbours: friendly, unfriendly, new, old, local gossips, reserved, eccentric, with secrets and possessions and dreams and relatives who visit.

51. Fancy dress: party, dance, hiring costumes, making costumes, ideas for fancy dress, using the cover of fancy dress to - — two people turning up in the same all covering costume…

52. Winter: storms, snow, blizzards, hailstorms, getting cut off, abandoning cars, being snowed in at a hotel, bitter cold, skiing, skating, walking, rescuing animals, rescuing people.

53. Spring: rain, flowers, soft evenings, lambs, birds nesting, daffodils, a time to be foolish?

54. Summer: hot lazy days, sudden storms, long warm evenings, holiday plans, gardening, sunbathing in gardens.

55. Autumn: brisk days, bonfires, Halloween, Firework Night, falling leaves, migrating birds.

56. Names: nicknames, funny names, odd names, invented names. What does a name mean and does the person match their name?

57. Play tourist in your own area! When did you last visit the tourist attractions locally and people watch in a different environment?

58. Birthdays: presents, parties, invitations, gifts (suitable and unsuitable!)

59. Cards: birthday, Christmas, wedding, christening, wrong cards for wrong occasions, or as happened once, young man rushing up the path with a card, wrong house…

60. Telephones: ringing, not ringing, interrupting, waiting for call, calls breaking long silences, distorted lines, crossed lines, joke calls from payphones, mobile phones, forgetting to charge them up, ringing at inappropriate times and places.
61. Answering machines, messages when you call, messages left, messages not recorded properly, messages not received.
62. Gyms: working out, losing flab, body building, aerobics, ladies in leotards, men in shorts, fit people, unfit people, personal trainers.
63. Sports: all kinds, indoors and out, opportunities for meeting people, socialising after games with people, club houses, showers, etc.
64. Drama societies: all those costumes, script meetings, rehearsals, backstage workers, dress rehearsals, reviews good and bad.
65. Photography: clubs setting particular themes for competitions, photographic expeditions, photographing wrong place at the wrong time…
66. Art classes often hire models for life classes. That could be interesting…
67. Luggage: stolen, broken, losing it, getting it back, coming open on the carousel, left luggage compartments, lost luggage departments, identical suitcases …
68. Restaurants: taking someone to dinner, good service, bad service, overdone music, overheard conversations, difficult diners, too much wine…
69. Christmas: presents, cards, buying gifts, family, friends, neighbours, or being alone, a thousand stories in Christmas alone.

70. Imagine being out of place, imagine being the odd one out at a large formal do, not sure of your etiquette, trying to follow others: stumbling by mistake into a church do, a Third Age person at a disco, anywhere a person would be out of place.

71. Moving: DIY moving, van hire, removal men, new neighbours, house problems, carpet laying, plumbing problems, items gone missing –

72. Food: cooking, storing, eating, overcooked, undercooked, gone off, loads of tales there.

73. Drink: soft drinks, fizzy drinks, alcoholic drinks, home-made wines, home-made lemonades and punch.

74. Entertainment industry: starlets, hopefuls, auditions, drama school, singing lessons, dancing lessons, elocution lessons.

75. Music industry: demos, gigs, music classes, classical music and orchestras, modern music and groups, groupies, recording industry, local bands.

You could also consider changing some of those locations to include:
Hospitals
Surgeries
Dentists
Law courts
Solicitors
Police and police stations
Every departure point there is, from ferries to airports – all have their own stories to tell.

Part Two

Things you need to explore and learn to do
to make your story/book richer, fuller in every way

Who will you meet on the way to Babylon?

I'm about to write a whole stack of stuff here that, if you were to take it literally, would mean you writing 800 page books... but that's not the point of the exercise. It's like having an iceberg floating toward you with 9/10ths of it below the waterline. If you know for sure how your character will react in any given situation, what they will be wearing, what job they came from, what car they drive... it will give you an immediate clue to how they will handle finding that dead body in their swimming pool or their one love in the arms of their bitterest enemy. I think that about sums it up...

Using this set of thoughts, you can make up character sheets and absorb the person's personality to the point when you will know what he will do next.

Writing fully rounded characters is a bit of an art form in itself. I'm coming back to the 'observe everything' topic again, it's the only way. People watching.

I take my Kindle with me everywhere, it's good cover for people watching and I do actually read the thing as well. But for me, the joy is running a second hand shop. I mean, where else do I get to observe the strange, the wonderful, the loving, the ordinary, the awkward, the tragic and the funny? There's the man who had a terrible accident on a building site, comes in on crutches, the man whose wife died of a cerebral haemorrhage whose granddaughter doesn't want the dolls and stuffed toys she collected. There are the obsessive collectors who want perfection in all they buy and there's the couples, long time married, the two moving and thinking as one, the banter, the loving jibes, the way they finish each other's sentences.

There's the funny things, the quirky things, the sheer idiotic things some people say, it all adds up to a rich panorama of people's personalities and abilities, all of which you will need, without realising it all the time, to make memorable characters.

Everything I see in the shop you can experience by observing people when you are out. How do they react to standing in a queue, not getting what they want from the shop, (run out, whatever) how are they in a supermarket with their trolley, pushy, aggressive, passive? How are they at the checkout, impatient, rude, charming; funny? What about at the petrol station, filling up with expensive fuel, or waiting to get to the pump? How do they react when their card is declined for whatever reason?

Which leads me to ATMs and customers in the bank... I could go on for hours. There are many, many places to observe your fellow man/woman/child. Be sure you get into the habit of watching and listening to them, it will enhance your characterisation skills considerably.

Illustrating traits can bring your characters to life in readers' minds more than a straightforward description. Think about wearing your characters' shoes to give your fiction a lifelike edge, think yourself into their lives. No matter how brief their appearance in a story or book, make them memorable. It will add to the story.

Let's get into this in more detail, shall we?

***

You're thinking hard about a storyline for a novel. You've got it all worked out, the family secrets buried in the mansion in deepest darkest Cornwall – or wherever. Fine, sounds interesting, but hold on, what about the people?

When you begin something as big as a novel, you would benefit from a little planning. Not the storyline, I hasten to add, unless you are the type of writer who needs a road map to get them to their destination, but planning your characters so you don't mix up ages, hair colour, skin colour, their abilities/disabilities... it's easy done.

You're thinking... I hope.

You have three genders to choose from, male/female/alien.

You have an age range of 0 to120 to choose from.

You can have them vertically challenged or towering above everyone or somewhere in the middle.

You can set them in just about any ethnic group there is and then some provided you know that group well enough to depict them with accuracy and compassion. That's important. If you want to step outside your ethnic group to write, be sure of your facts and feelings.

Physically, they have to be pretty normal, unless you've chosen to go the Hunchback of Notre Dame or alien route. So, apart from the odd quirk, (missing finger, hare lip as in Precious Bane) or anything else that makes them different, your real characterisation is in their personality, speech, likes and dislikes and everything that makes them human. Or alien, if your aliens have personalities.

Let's think about that personality bit, what makes the person different from everyone else. What makes you different from everyone else? There has to be a bit of you in there somewhere, it's hard to write without including our own feelings/prejudices/likes/dislikes/etc.

Do you get the feeling some people arrive in this world with a giant chip on their shoulder which the nursing staff managed to miss where others seem to arrive with a smile and you know their life will be sunshine from end to end?

Somewhere along the line some people's personality changes for the better/worse because of a 'happening', accident, illness, family breakup, bereavement… sometimes it brings out the best in people, sometimes it brings out the worst.

Think about the many faces of the people you know and remember, when writing, no one is the same as the person next to them, even though they might be identical in age, weight, location and everything. Their thoughts, their hatreds, their obsessions, their loves, their needs, are entirely different.

Two people can look at the same incident/parade/landscape and come away with entirely different perspectives of what they had just seen.

This is why I can think up a simple theme for an anthology and have the widest possible range of stories come in where each other has 'seen' the theme differently.

Diversity is everything and the key to interesting writing.

Children
aka rug-monkeys, offspring, nuisances and a hundred other names as they grow

What can children do for your book? How can they enliven it, how can they enhance it and enchant the reader? My short story example was a boy but even earlier than that, they have their own enchantment, as witnessed by the visit the shop had one day. A man came in with a very young girl, maybe three at the most.

'I want a teddy!'

Well, she would, we had a surfeit of them at the time, it was a kid's paradise.

Dad: 'no, you already had two today.'

By this time she was walking around clutching a bear.

'I want a teddy!'

'No, you already had two today.'

Teddy thrown violently back into the chair. Sulky face. My partner took pity on her and offered money to buy sweets. She came over and took it, then ran back to her father and, in a very loud stage whisper, said:

'The man said I could take a teddy when I leave.'

Imagine what that child would be like when she gets just a little older. I imagined her parents were going to have serious problems...

Children come with their own dreams, desires and agendas. They aren't always the same as ours. It

would be a mistake to think that way. Get inside the head of a child; remember how you were back then.
   If you can!

We are what we remember

This came to me one night when I was thinking about another section of this book: sounds/music = time machine. I thought about music and sounds that instantly took me back many years and realised that the sum total of a person is their memories. How many times during a conversation that ranges outside politics and finances does someone say 'I always remember…' or simply 'I remember when… (not sure if that first one is an Isle of Wight saying, we have a lot of them…)

So, I remember when… life was better, things were cheaper, police were respected, vandalism wasn't so rampant and murderers got caught. Oh, and we measured things in imperial not decimal.

I'm simplifying a bit, but thinking on the many conversations in the shop, not that much simpler. When writing of the 'elderly' remember they live in the past so you need to slant their dialogue accordingly.

Teens, same thing. They already have several years of experience behind them, the torments of school with all its rigid unspoken rules and pecking order, those who were 'in', those on the periphery and those who were always the last ones to be chosen for teams. The fat ones, the 'disabled' (spectacles, hearing aids, health problems) the 'nerds' who only wanted to learn. Your characters, if they are teens and upwards, have a personality coloured by what they remember. Do they need to take revenge on a cruel world because they were bullied by both pupils and teachers sometimes? What of those who were dyslexic and no one knew, so they were labelled 'slow' or 'dim' or just 'difficult'? This spills into who we are in our later life. This colours the decisions we make, the pathways we choose, the career we end up in, the friends we attract and so... of necessity this colours the way the person speaks, acts and moves in your story or book.

My midnight thoughts, this ended up as midnight musings, revealed something I had overlooked completely. I lived a solitary childhood, always on my own, ranging freely in the local park with our dog by my side, sitting under a huge oak, finding the acorn cups and marvelling at them, visiting the library for yet more books to read, trying to translate the chalk marks on fence posts and pavements to see if there were messages for spies or other people... and asked myself: was it any wonder I ended up as a writer?

We are what we remember. If you dig into your memories, your past, see where you came from, what moulded you into what you are now, who you are now (the two are very different, says me and so will you, if you think about it) and write some of that longing, that innocence, that need to know and the fun you had into your books and stories, especially books, they will really begin to come alive.

Learning to listen...

"I think it was all 1960 and that summer went on for a space of years, held magically intact in a web of sounds; the sweet hum of crickets, the machine-gun roar of playing-cards riffling against the spokes of some kid's bicycle as he pedalled home for a late supper of cold cuts and iced tea..."
Stephen King, 'The Body'.

It's been said one of the greatest time machines of all is music. Instant transportation back to that time; that place, that person, that event. 'Remember when...' but there are other sounds, as Stephen King explores in his story of youth, friendship and discovery with his reminiscing of the summer of 1960. Where were you as a teen? What memories does music evoke for you and in you? Good, bad, indifferent, all music has its links in our past. It isn't only songs, either; it's theme tunes to certain programmes on the radio, before TV took over our lives (those of us old enough to remember and have lived through those times. For the youngsters out there, it's old TV programmes and advertisements which will trigger the memories, yes?)
For me it was Radio Luxemburg and hits, David Jacobs introducing Journey Into Space on the radio, the sound of my Dad cutting the lawn and tending the garden (which he did endlessly) or the rhythmic chopping sound as he mixed cement for yet another project, that's when he wasn't DIY-ing, as in

wallpapering and painting – which leads into another section which we will reach shortly.

You'll have your own memories, brought back by your experiences at certain times relating to certain music. The sounds of events in your life will stay with you as they do with me: the thunk of a car door, the sound of rain on the window or the roof, water dripping through trees as we buried my much loved grandfather. The sharp bark of a dog we all adored, the chattering of the budgie who defied all the odds and lived to be 17. Explore your memories, your experiences with 'sound' in all its forms, natural and man-made. See where it takes you.

Then wrap that into your writing.

We all live with that instant time machine. Don't overlook it.

What's in a name?

Just about everything.

Your characters need the right names. Names define people. Names give the reader a clue as to the character of the person they are reading about. Names follow fashions (how many Harpers, a la the Beckhams, are there going to be in the near future…?) and you need to watch for that.

Sixties names tend to be Tracy and Stacey and Sharon and… you get the general idea, I'm sure. I know a lot of Brians. They tend to be in their sixties, along with the Steves and Daves and Phils. Loads of them. John appears to be timeless and universal, along with Jack. Parents seem to be more imaginative with their girls than their sons but I do know some with odd offbeat names and wonder how that will affect their futures –did River Phoenix find his name a liability when growing up?

Find your names from a baby name book, because they give you the meanings. These can give a lot of information by themselves. Watch for ethnic names, you'll know them when you see them, without me insulting any particular group in this handbook…sensibilities are easily offended… and choose the names with care, even for a short story. About thirty years back I read a short story in a woman's magazine where the heroine was Elsie. It seemed horribly wrong, outdated, a name for an elderly person. Now, thirty years on, the name is being introduced again, there are at least two babies

I know of named Elsie. But... in the intervening period there doesn't seem to be any.

One way of checking names is to listen to mothers calling their wayward ones. I've heard Dennis and Albert recently, a Stanley too. Charles appears to have become Charlie, Alfred has changed to Alfie. As the language modifies itself, so names undergo changes. Be aware of it and use it.

When writing my novel 'Forever', I checked everything with great care. The book covers the years 495 AD to 1995 AD, so I needed a lot of names. I discovered oddities such as the name Daniel disappearing for upwards of two hundred years. No reason was given. Biblical names usually survive whilst other fashionable ones come and go but that one went walkabout. The name Guy disappeared for the longest time after the ill-fated Guy Fawkes was executed. Things like that affect the popularity of names. You can imagine how many George's there are already since Prince George made his appearance in our world...

Remember how names are contracted, too, Derek becomes Del, Terry, already reduced from Terence, becomes Tel, Alan is Al, Michelle is invariably Meech, Tracy is Trace, it goes on. For me, on a strictly personal level, the contraction of the lovely name Olwen to Ollie is unforgiveable...but people tend to do that. My name is rarely chopped up; it's actually changed rather than altered. At work and for a lot of people I am simply Dee. That suits me better than Dot or Dottie, which I dislike. It doesn't suit me. (One book said to be called Dorothy meant you had a Scottish grandmother. I did.)

Contractions can be used to an advantage in a story or book, though. Chris or Pat, male or female? You will know quite a few names that could be used either way. That could provide a twist or two.

Match the first and last names carefully too. There again, picking the right name could make or break the character. Too posh a name for a working class person will ruin what you are building, unless it is done intentionally to provide conflict for your people.

It's not really a minefield; it's a good way of building people. Names can be lifted from many places, magazines, advertising leaflets, even road signs. Be aware all the time of what you are looking at. People watching, everything watching. You're a writer. Be conscious of all you see.

The way we look

This is the tough one to get into a story without overdoing it. The normal reaction is: he stood 5' 10, bulky body, heavily muscled arms; strong stern face with an oft broken nose and lips that seemed ashamed or incapable of smiling.

That lot is no more than a bunch of clichés. There are better ways – but then, there always is.

He was taller than me and I touched the average at 5 -8 or so. The difference was, he carried more bulk than me and his nose said he had won (or lost) more fights than I had.

Better? Takes a bit of thinking but that's what writing's all about. Thinking.

Whether to be 'nice' or outright bitchy depends on your character's view of others. Does he hate the world and everyone in it? If so, overweight people are plain fat, disabled become crisps and the beautiful are admired from a distance because for people like that, they are usually out of their league (unless they are rolling rich, of course.)

Does he love the world and everyone in it? Then overweight people are happy in their chubbiness, disabled are to be helped or at least treated as normal and the beautiful are within arm's reach, all he has to do is make the effort, rich or not.

Or is he totally indifferent to someone's looks? The acne-riddled teen doesn't bother him, although it bothers the teen more than you can believe if you've not been that bad with it.

Does he ignore specs? This, in our house, is an ongoing thing. By lengthy observation we have come to see that, for the wider world, people who wear spectacles are the geeks, the nerds, the plain ones. Where did we get this from? In the newspaper's female section they do makeovers. The woman is always, without fail, shown as wearing spectacles in the 'before' photo and contacts in the 'after' one. Criminals who are cursed with short sight are referred to as 'bespectacled'. That is applied to a whole load of people, but we did notice that it is always mentioned when someone's arrested, for whatever reason. As if it makes any difference to what they did. Ugly Betty wears spectacles. 'Bespectacled' is not only a clumsy word, it also condemns the wearer to the tag for the rest of their lives. So, kids who have to wear them at school, are condemned to being 'specky', 'four-eyes' and all manner of other names. Something else to consider when writing about looks.

It can work the other way. I saw someone today wearing gorgeous spectacles with gold coloured frames. It's what I want next time I get to buy some. I tend to admire spectacles more than outfits; it's just the way it is with me… they can be a very big fashion accessory for your characters.

Cosmetics. Used sparingly, overdone, lipstick too bright? This can apply to both genders, there are some transvestites who know just what they're doing and others who go OTT and ruin the effect.

Hair colour. Just about anything goes these days; I've seen all colours except custard yellow, I think. You can change a person by their hair colour alone; it could also affect their personality. Those who are brown who become blonde often become more outgoing and confident. Hair styles affect the way people look, too. I have long hair, I would look completely different now with an 'old lady' crop (which is why I won't do it!) with a blue or purple rinse… no thanks!

Tattoos, everyone seems to be sporting the things. Does your character have a colourful display everywhere? And has he regretted it? I know one person who has facial tattoos he seriously regrets now he is older and wiser. Does he or doesn't he have them?

Body and face piercing. Yes? No? Lip, nose, eyebrow, ears, everywhere else… body piercing is as common as tattoos these days. Don't overlook it.

Also, what effect does face piercing have on the person? Someone who works locally has the bridge of her nose, her eyebrow and lip pierced. Sometimes she goes without the piercings, just leaving the holes. Which is worse? Would you prefer to see the piercings or the holes or are you put off by either/or?

It's part of life. Deal with it in your stories. It adds colour and authenticity to your people.

The way we walk

Walking. Something we do naturally from an early age but which few people take much notice of until you begin to watch the way they do it.

Examples: The woman walking along in front of me had a casual, easy almost sexy sway to her body. I had the sudden odd thought that she was at peace with her shape and it showed in the way she moved. Both of us left the side road and went out into the main street. Coming down the road toward me was a smartly dressed woman, boots with heels, black woollen coat flying in the wind, texting as she walked, iPod earpieces showing. Her walk said, 'I am important!' as those boot heels clicked on the paving stones.

The old man, who spends time every morning standing in a doorway smoking a cigarette, slowly shambled up the hill in front of me, shoulders hunched, ageing revealed in every line of his body. The young mother pushing the buggy down the road showed every sign of weariness in her movements, her steps faltered, there was nothing positive about her at all and it wasn't even 9am.

When people watching, be sure to observe the way they walk. You can tell so much from body language when people are on the move.

You might already know the old lady with curvature of the spine, who of necessity has to walk slowly. Her condition won't let her do otherwise, but you also know she seeks sympathy and attention, almost demanding people stop and talk to her. She loves to window shop and often stops to look at things she obviously has no intention of buying, such as expensive jewellery or fancy lamps for the home.

There's the young man with the stiff right leg which he 'throws' a little as he walks. You know it's a false limb; you've watched him progress from wheelchair through crutches and walking stick to confident stride, apart from that slightly odd movement which clicks the limb and allows him to take the step. Would others know from the walk?

Large busty ladies walk proudly, thrusting their assets in front of them, parting the waves of people like a figurehead. Slim ladies walk delicately, usually wearing heels, strappy sandals mostly, and wrap themselves in fashionable draped scarves. Men with large paunches also tend to part the waves of people, but more in a 'barrel of beer' style, rolling their way down the road. Slim men tend to almost flaunt themselves, but not quite, as if to say, 'look at me, I don't come into the 'obese' statistics, do I?'

Lovers walk close together, sharing secrets by touch as well as by words. Third Age people with walking sticks walk hesitantly sometimes, hanging on to their partners, afraid of letting go, perhaps as much spiritually as physically.

The unique characteristics of a person's walk were highlighted by my daughter. She said no matter what shoes I am wearing (as a shoeaholic it could be any of the 50 or so pairs I own) she knows it is me walking up the road from the car park, no matter how many others are also walking up the road or have walked up the road. She knows when it's me. Then my business partner said 'I would know your footsteps anywhere.'

I don't know what it is, I thought I put one foot in front of the other (usually in heels, nothing else will do – or used to be, now arthritis changes both the walk and the footwear) but the thought stayed with me: if I have a distinctive walk, then so does everyone else. Finding the walk for your characters, pinning it down and utilising it in a story or novel, could help bring that character alive even more than the standard description could.

We are how we walk, as much as we are how we speak, think, act and react.

Try some 'people-watching' from the point of view of the way they walk. A café or coffee bar is an ideal place to do this, if you sit in the window and just quietly observe. It's enlightening and could be enriching for your writing, too.

The way we talk: Estuary, anyone?

For those who may not know, Estuary is the name given to the accent of those who pretty much live alongside the Thames as it heads from London into Essex and the open sea. It's Cockney but with a slur, a sliding way of talking that is often taken for laziness. It defines the Essex person completely. If you've seen The Only Way Is Essex you'll know what I mean.

The way we talk is also indicative of our upbringing and where we come from. (Two different things.) Memories of working with someone who had an unusual accent, she was Rhodesian, back when it was Rhodesia. The States give us a variety of American accents, the UK does the same. There is the lilt of the Welsh, the rhythmic Irish, the harsher Scots, the often unintelligible northern counties, Manchester, Birmingham, Nottingham, all have their own accents.

London is a mix of them all, including the ethnic population busy adding itself to the glory that is the English language.

Teens will use the current street slang, be sure to check that out, it changes all the time, almost by the week, it seems. 60s 'youth' will still say things are 'cool'. War veterans will use Army slang. Criminals invariably use bad language, but the level of that is where the line needs to be drawn. That's fine in dialogue, try not to use it outside that, there's no need to use it as a description. That's just overload and stories don't benefit from overload.

Remember to write speech idiosyncrasies into your writing. The zombie in The Skullface Chronicles constantly says 'for sure' to the annoyance of the sane part of his brain which keeps telling him to 'give over with the 'for sure's.' It's something he does. Your character will have a speech affectation that defines him. You'll find it if you work at it.

Apparently, despite being Essex girl to my bones, no one can detect an accent. It throws a lot of people, I'm pleased to say. It's nice being different...

Growing up...

Wanted child, unwanted child, only child, one of two, one of three, one of a big family. And his childhood generally, freedom to roam, cosseted by overbearing parents, ignored by them as he wasn't wanted, wrong sex child, they wanted a boy and got a girl... friends, no friends, bully, bullied, left out of party invites, not chosen for team games, loved by grandparents, aunts and all or not a favoured grandchild/whatever. All this makes a difference. Big family background, no family background.

Example. My mother's family was large; she had seven sisters and one brother. They all, if they could, went to Grandmother's every Saturday. So us kids grew up with this motley collection of uncles, aunts and cousins in a big loving easy-going atmosphere. Other people I know hardly saw their aunts and uncles, where mine were so much a part of my life. One Aunt helped make my wedding dress, an uncle took the photos; another did the flowers... I borrowed my grandmother's ring for the 'something borrowed' item. What if I had not had that big family around me during my formative years? What sort of person would I be now?

It's family which colours a person, in addition to their inbuilt character. Consider it.

And pets? We always had dogs. We had budgies. We had chickens. Your character grew up with... none of that? Is he afraid of dogs, prefers cats because they make fewer demands on you? Keeps a parrot or some other exotic bird or more than that, a reptile of some kind? The animal your character favours shows another side of him, too.

Schooling, public or state? Someone I know lived on an estate not known for its money or ability to produce public schoolboy standards. He was sent to an elite school. He didn't fit there and he didn't fit with his friends on the estate, either. It made a big impact on his growing up. What's your character's background with school?

Is he a good time keeper or is he consistently late for everything, appointments, meals, meeting up with friends...

It's amazing how much of all of this is out there – I'm talking of people I know, not inventing these scenarios. Any one of them, with the right twist, is the basis for your serial killer, your champion of the fair ladies, the hermit; the high flyer who makes up the basis of your novel/story.

An Exotic Pet Supply shop opened up here on the island, it seems to be thriving... how many odd people are there living here... or shouldn't I even begin to ask that question...

Food, glorious food

Unless the chef, the meal, the dessert and the wine is an integral part of your story, don't go there. Pack everyone off to a restaurant and pick it up again when they've done eating. Sometimes it works, sometimes it's even necessary, (in IT they have their serious 'shall we do this' discussion around the waitress coming in and out, often disrupting what someone's saying and then there's the horror of the fortune cookies at the end. Without the preliminaries that wouldn't work. A classic example of a novelist completely at home with his craft.)

Another thriller which arrived was weighed down with cooking from the start. He's in the kitchen rustling up this that and the other and nowhere could I see that it was necessary to the storyline. It didn't even make me hungry, as I don't overly care about eating anyway. I'm not alone in this feeling, so when you're tempted to give your reader a cordon bleu menu, ease back; be considerate, we don't all want all the details. Wine snobs can get their kicks from wine magazines, not from thrillers or other stories. Refer to some priceless bottle of something or other and it will go over the head of 7/8ths of your readers, starting with me. Use the available space to do something more interesting: move the story on. You may 'lose' a couple of hundred words here and there, better that than lose a reader. I didn't get further than the first chapter of that thriller.

Clothes maketh the man (or woman)

You've worked out what your characters look like; now take another step into finding out more about them. Look in their wardrobe. What can you see?

Clothes maketh the man. Old proverb and a true one. People who care about themselves wear assertive clothes, suits, dresses, skirts, smart coats, smart shoes, nice jewellery. Those who don't slob around in jeans, sweatshirts, hoodies, trainers, both sexes. Clothes are a clear indication of the personality of the person wearing them. You know that yourself, if you look at someone and they resemble a homeless person, you very likely have less time for them than you would the smart businessman who appears to be lost.

That's the stereotyping taken care of.

Now think about what would happen if one of the yuppies decided to go the slob-wear route.

What about a woman, normally a power dresser, going into hippie style clothes and sandals? What is that saying about her state of mind?

Teens, you can ignore them in this regard, they wouldn't be seen dead on the street in anything but the latest fad, even if that fad is jeans hanging half way down their thighs…

Children tend to follow fashion trends if their families can afford the clothes. Otherwise, we are talking charity shops and hand-me-downs; take some time out to consider how that goes down with the older children. Not very well, mostly.

You need to wrap the clothes into the physical appearance when describing someone without labouring the point that you are describing someone. It can be done but we are back to 'thinking' again, rather than just rushing through the story.

Ongoing thoughts... if you watch old films, old documentaries, you will see people wearing hats. Men rarely went out without a trilby; women had their variety of hats. This thought came to me recently when I caught part of a Western on TV. The cowboys were scrambling to get away from the gunslinger, but still had to go back and rescue their Stetsons... hats were important. Don't forget them. They're an integral part of the whole clothes scene. I know this came up earlier in the book but it's there and it's important and it matters.

Fresh back from lunch with more of that 'observe everything' edict going on. At the counter, paying for his meal, was a tall, rangy guy wearing solid workman jeans, rivets and all, a tad too large, the material sort of sagged a bit round the hips, some kind of sweat shirt despite the warm day, worn old body-warmer, worn old shoes. He looked a part of his clothes and they looked a part of him. I tried to picture him scrubbed up in a suit and failed.

A young couple took his table. They had a 13 month old baby with them (she said so to the waitress) who was wearing a dark blue sweat shirt and solid looking jeans...

Images like this burn into the mind, if you are observant enough, they linger, they emerge later on to add colour to a scene. That kind of contrast must happen fairly often but it happened right there for me today and today I am working on the handbook, so…

The labourer is worth his hire

Most of us go to work. Our employment is, in many ways, defined by who we are – so I guess I need to use that dreaded word 'class' here. Of course some brave determined people break out of their 'working class' mould and hit the big time. They are the source of some good novels and real life books, too. But on the whole, people are defined by their upbringing and environment as to the job they do. The service industry would be hard put to function without the people who live on estates, in social housing or whatever, as would the health services who rely on cleaners, porters, drivers, clerks and the like who support the nurses and doctors. We need people to do those jobs every bit as much as we need people to tend to our health, our teeth, our banking needs and all the other 'high flyer' industries, including Government.

It seems blatantly obvious when set out like that, but once again, it needs adding into the mix that is your character. What he does defines what he wears, where he lives, how he spends his time and, more than anything, how he speaks.

If music be the food of love...

What music does your character like? Is he a heavy metal freak or is he into the ballads of Abba and the Carpenters? Or is she into Abba and the Carpenters? Teens will follow current fashion in music as they do with clothes and street slang.

What about their love of live music, festivals, evening gigs, local groups in pubs or playing at weddings or parties?

The variety of music available is immense, from classical and opera through to rap, hip-hop and R&B. Match the music to the person. It all adds something.

One day a guy came in the shop wearing a Guns 'N' Roses tee-shirt, then someone wearing one with the image of the King on it. Two days later a Fleetwood Mac fan walked in. This tendency to broadcast your musical tastes/heroes to the world does make for interesting and varied tee-shirt reading. It also surprises me when someone who looks as if he should be doing the whole heavy metal bit buys the Billy Joel CD we had in the shop forever...

I saw a 'poster' on line recently, which said *don't judge a book by its movie.*

I have to say *don't judge a music buyer by their tee-shirt...*

But it's something else to consider, someone looking so unlike the type for the music they like, a C&W fan without the waistcoat, cowboy boots and jeans, for example. It's all something to add to the mix, to develop the character without giving everything away.

What do you believe?

The Jehovah's Witnesses called by again the other day, with their magazines and invitations to attend their meetings at Kingdom Hall. Sometimes I am polite, sometimes I just say 'I'm a Spiritualist' and they run as if I'm the devil incarnate. My beliefs sometimes colour my writing, if it goes in that direction. Mostly, though, I work at keeping spiritualism out of it, as it isn't a belief that goes down well with everyone...

So, what does your character believe? Which church do they belong to, either for religious reasons or for appearances' sake? A conventional church, Church of England, Methodist, Catholic, you know all the usual ones. If they are a member of a church, are they overtly Christian, wearing a cross or the 'fish' design, or have it on their car as a sticker? Do they go regularly, does the female character go to any groups, help with the flowers, wash the floor occasionally, sort hymn books... (Been there, done all that.) It can throw up some interesting sidelines, actually. Remembering a time when the church I attended went in with the other three in the town, United Reform, Catholic and Methodist, to stage a big flower festival. We chose as the theme the course of a life. United Reform ended up with death - and I would have thought – resurrection. What we got was 'so after that, then, nothing, I guess.' Huh? So much for belief! Again, a look into someone's psyche. Comments like that reveal so much about someone.

Are they secretly into witchcraft, Paganism, or just plain atheism at a time when it isn't acceptable to be an atheist?

A lot depends on the era in which you set the storyline but it is there, it is part of us, it defines us. Get admitted to hospital and right after name, address, date of birth, they ask 'what religion are you?'

At the end of the working day/week...

In your character's spare time, what do they like to do? Read, knit, crochet, carve, paint, write, DIY, fix cars and motorbikes, take their dog for a walk, tend their cat/bird/chicken/ horse …

What sport do they like/follow? Do they play a sport, go to stadiums, have a season ticket for a series, buy memorabilia, wear the scarf, fly the flag… all this adds to their background, their way of seeing things, reacting to things, accepting things, handling things.

The stay-at-home people tend to be the true homemakers, baking, making, sewing, knitting, gardening, DIY-ing, washing and polishing the family car, sweeping the pavement…

Shopping? There is a lot to notice in the way people shop, impulse buy, careful buy, disappearing into the changing rooms with three items at a time, watching the pennies, flashing the credit cards, browsing the books and magazines for hours.

Grocery shopping, that bane of everyone's life, trolleys piled high with – one trolley I saw a while back was full to overflowing with sliced loaves. Go speculate. From small peeks into someone's life like that can come a story or a vignette for your novel, another aspect to someone's character. From the shoppers, the floor walkers, the shelf stockers, the Internet shoppers to the check out attendants, supermarkets are a veritable mine of hints, glimpses and sometimes full blown story ideas.

Vroom! Vroom!

The shopping is loaded into – a car which again will match the person. The high flyer will want a flashy car with a prestigious badge on the front, the teen boy racers want something fast and flashy which can be crashed if necessary – and often is – young women want something smart and reliable. I'm not stereotyping too much here, again this is observation. I park in a public car park; I see all sorts of cars and all sorts of people getting into and out of those cars. I can often match the people walking in with car keys in their hands and the car I see across the parking bays. You can do this; it's back to observation again. Watch: observe everything, from the way people eat in restaurants and greasy spoon cafés to how they roll down the street at night when they've run out of money or the capacity to drink any more. How someone drives comes into that as well as what they drive.

So… do they drive with one foot on the brake for the last moment near-collision, is there road rage from the moment the car door slams, is there a confrontational attitude to pedestrians and cyclists and wildlife?

Do they adhere to every speed limit, not cross a single white line; always stop at amber, wave politely to all others who allow them free passage when there are blockages along the road?

Are they confident, nervous, fresh out of driving school and scared stiff or massively arrogantly confident and heading for a disaster straight off?

Driving matches the house and the car and the hobbies. It is all part of one. Driving is an essential part of our lives; don't let that get away from you.

What did you do in the war, Daddy?

Is there any family anywhere not touched by a war of some kind? The big world wars, either they were fighting men, or they were rejected as not fit to fight. Both ways were bad, both ways affected the families of the men concerned. Moving on, Falklands, Iraq, Gulf, Vietnam, Afghanistan… what did your hero do during the war and, if he isn't old enough to be a fighting man, what did his father and grandfather do? War stories permeate a family's history, not to be escaped and definitely not to be overlooked.

The big World Wars split families, lost us a generation of young men. But… this is not unusual. In researching the Woodville family ('my' period of history is the Wars of the Roses, when the Woodvilles were a leading family in England) I came across the story of the ill-fated campaign led by Sir Edward Woodville who took 440 men from the Isle of Wight to Brittany to fight the French. Only one boy came back with the news of the slaughter of the entire contingent of men. Apart from the sorrow generated by such a loss, the removal from the island of that complete generation of workers, farmers, farm hands, you name it, must have set the island economy back by about 100 years. War at any time in history is destructive in the extreme. 28,000 men died at Towton 550 years ago. 28,000 men in ten hours of hand to hand fighting. How many able bodied people were left to carry on?

Man has always fought wars, sought to start wars and, in many ways, to benefit from them. Once a war is on the horizon, a country's economy begins to move upwards, uniforms, arms, vehicles, supplies, are commissioned and some people get to make a lot of money. It can be very useful to remember this when writing your war stories – and you will, for there are many tales to be told about and around and in the many, many wars this earth has endured.

Tidy room, tidy mind – perhaps?

Is your character one of life's tidy people, ever putting things away, or someone who throws things and doesn't worry where they land? This trait can drive others mad, a good point of conflict for a story, even as background to the main conflict you set up.

Likewise, if I might slide it in here, dirty or clean? Some people are fanatical about cleanliness, showering all the time, changing their clothes all the time where others seem to be indifferent to the needs of hygiene. It all adds to character. Think about it when you're writing.

OCD anyone? That too can make or break a person and delineate a character too. Everyone has some degree of it; it's those who allow it to rule their lives who are the really colourful ones. Something to think on.

A brush with the Law

So, your character runs up against the police. How does he react to this? Does being arrested bother him? Has he a pet lawyer on the end of the telephone? Is he outraged, angry, anxious? If whatever it is comes to court, how does he handle the cross-examination by people who are paid to make mincemeat of him? This says a lot about someone's personality and, more than that, the other people who are affected, those who have to visit him, those who have to attend court, those who visit him in prison (if it gets that far…) wrap all this into your character profile. It will be very revealing. People react in vastly different ways when they confront Authority.

A Sense of Place
The right setting for your characters

'Joby's studio apartment was four flights up in a converted Victorian hotel with cracked Tiffany windows, scarred parquet floors and beamed ceilings enameled in garish yellow. It shared a wall with the moldering Art Deco movie theatre next door, so that late at night, if he pressed his ear to the plaster, he could hear snatches of sweaty passion or melancholy dialogue in foreign languages.'
The Book of Joby by Mark J Ferrari.

Joby's life is scarred by virtue of his being the chosen one in a wager between God and Lucifer, a life that sends him to different locations and, consequently, various 'homes'. Each time Mark J Ferrari manages, with a few deft words, to evoke a sense of place for his hero. On this particular occasion the apartment is shabby, noisy and affordable only if he stops eating.

We all live somewhere, even if it is on the street. The homeless of my home town have deep shop doorways to shelter in. The rest of the town is divided unequally between blocks of flats, tiny matchbox houses, large once ornate beautiful houses divided into apartments, bungalows, cottages and standard 'three bedrooms with bay window in lounge' type houses. Every one is different, because the people who live in them are different. But – have you noticed how certain areas draw people to them: the most conscientious of council tenants often share their estate with families who decorate their front gardens with wrecked cars, rusting toys and a sufficient variety of weeds to keep a botanist happy for hours. A housing estate draws in young people with families, reasonably neat and tidy properties, open plan gardens; the occasional buggy left in a doorway to indicate a small person lives there. The posh houses, where the more affluent live, have the hanging baskets, the roses over the porch, the discreet satellite dish and the well polished car in the driveway. The really expensive areas just smell of money.

We make our own 'nest' and furnish it in our own way. Writers have as many different working environments as there are writers... from Spartan to cluttered, with everything in between. So, when considering your character(s), think how and where they would live. Mr and Mrs Suburban would have one of the three-bed-lounge-with-bay-window type houses, the elderly have retired to bungalows, the young at heart have the cottages, the aspiring youngsters have the flats and tiny matchbox houses - or are we stereotyping people by saying this? Would it make a difference to Mr and Mrs Suburban if they lived in a tiny picturesque cottage in one of the side roads where cars can't go and everyone knows everyone? Or would they prefer a bungalow even though they aren't elderly?

If you wish to set an instant scenario for your reader, the stereotype works well. The one good thing about stereotypes is that you don't need to use many words to set the scene for your reader - a depiction of a standard three-bed house, freshly painted, snow white nets at the window, an immaculate front garden, closely mowed lawn and not a leaf to disturb the path, will tell your reader immediately the type of person who lives there without you dwelling on it. Once inside, add the laser lamp, the print of the Chinese girl or the crying boy and the picture is complete without another word being added. It leaves you free to concentrate on the story.

If you want to give a twist to your character, take them out of their 'normal' expected environment and set them in something entirely different, to give them a bit more of a challenge. What if the immaculate front garden and freshly painted exterior hid an interior more befitting a Goth or punk? Black walls, heavy drapes, blood red lamps, your imagination could run wild and fit the place out to resemble the Hellfire Club on a bad night. It would give your characters a whole new dimension.

The trick really is not to stereotype. Sometimes you need to be outrageous and adventurous in your writing. Take your characters out of their staid environment, set them in a new place where they need to re-evaluate their lives, give them new challenges and see what transpires. We need a sense of place for ourselves and for our heroes and heroines too.

Senses – we have them, so use them!

We all have five –sometimes six – senses. Your characters – unless you write in a disability – have sight, hearing, speech, touch, taste. Any or all of these can be drawn in to create meaningful living people.

Sight. If we were to lose that we would lose so much, from the obvious, rainbows and sunsets and flowers and landscapes, to the smile of the one you love and the sea rolling in on a beach. Obvious statement, I know that, but sometimes we take these things for granted. Where would I be without the gift of sight which allows me to read, endlessly, to write to everyone, endlessly, to drive, to photograph, to walk around and not need someone to lead me? I can fall quite easily even with sight, heaven help me if I had no sight…

Hearing. Not to hear music again would be – unbelievable. I live with music in my car. Turn the key, the CD comes on. (In the car at the moment, the King, the King and more King. Sometimes its Four Tops, Four Tops and more Four Tops. In the door compartment is Neil Diamond's Tap Root Manuscript, with one special song on it that cuts through to the heart. When I want deep emotions, I play that track. Also there is The Doors, the brooding enigmatic genius Jim Morrison doing Rider On The Storm, surely the ultimate horror song. Yes? Music, takes me to and from work and on long journeys to the other side of the island to visit friends. Not to hear voices again, not to hear laughter, birds, water – which almost has its own language when it chuckles its way over rocks and stones.

Speech. Covered this already but it is a sense and to lose it, as we do when we get a filthy cold and have laryngitis, creates all manner of problems. Useful in a story.

Touch. What do things feel like... upholstery, silk, woollen clothes, the fur of a dog or cat, the chill of the metalwork of your car, the feel of the keys in your hand. The delicate texture of a baby's skin, the roughness of an outdoor worker's hands. The comfort of hot water when showering or bathing, the luxury of a fluffy towel. It's also the sensation of feeling: the wind buffeting you, the lightness of snow, the sharpness of hail, the gentleness of a summer shower, the drenching coldness of a winter one. Touch. It's everything.

Taste. Your character can delight in the smell of coffee, which someone said is a drink which smells better than it tastes, the richness of the coffee in his mouth, or be repelled by the bitterness of it, his taste buds rejecting it, whilst his hand finds the cup too hot. It's easy when you work at it...

The sixth sense is when you bring in the psychic ability we all have but so few of us use. Having said that, you know well when someone is looking/staring at you, even if you have your back to them. You are aware of people's animosity even when they're smiling with their teeth and even their eyes. You understand these things on a basic survival level and that's the sixth sense that can be of great use in your story/novel.

Owner of a broken heart...

One essential to remember when writing about 'people', i.e. human beings with all their foibles, they FEEL.

And so... anger, sorrow, jealousy, spite, grief, hatred, envy, joy, peace, torment, anxiety, anticipation, expectation, disappointment...

Our early years are spent working out how to manipulate parents and others into giving us sweets, money and anything else we can cadge in exchange for a hug, a kiss and a smile. It changes when we go to school, then we have to cope with others who are just as manipulative in getting their own way with school work, with lunch money, with being chosen for teams...

Teen years are full of angst, broken relationships, misunderstandings; arguments with just about everyone.

Later years we run into the biggies, partners, babies, home making, home breaking, divorce, being alone, trying to find a new partner, learning to be single; learning to be a widow/widower.

How does your character handle sex, if you will excuse the pun? Is he a user, taking but not giving, is he a considerate lover, an adventurous one, a conservative one? Does he like to experiment, would he experiment?

All of this changes the person in some way each time it happens. Bring it into the writing. Don't leave anything out that might touch your reader and demand they follow your story to the end.

Where does it hurt?

One thought invariably leads to another... and that section led to thinking about pain, illness, suffering.

The doctor's surgery is a good place to people-watch. Incidentally I have been bursting, almost literally, to find out the end result of the small saga I witnessed last time I was there.

An ultra bossy woman stalked in, no other word for it, followed by a very meek cowed obviously bullied much older woman. When the name was called, Ms Bossy got up and said 'is it all right if I come in with my mother? I know the story better than she does.' (me thinking, I bet you do...)

When they came out, Ms Bossy was stamping rather than stalking, with poor mother trailing along behind. As they reached the exit I heard 'Well, now we know the REAL story, don't we?" and they were gone.

Suggestions as to what lay behind that particular family drama on a postcard, please... It's that kind of incident that makes for fascinating storyline thoughts.

Back to the thoughts. In a surgery waiting room you can identify the single mothers, the worried over anxious ones, the elderly with genuine fear written on their faces, the cadgers...

All this is repeated in hospital, in A&E especially but don't disregard wards, clinics, waiting rooms... all need to be considered at some time. There's both sides to think about. The last time I went there with my daughter on an appointment, the receptionist was busy on her phone with what was obviously a personal call. She ended it, looked at us and said "I'm off duty now." Thanks, we thought...we feel reassured, cared for, considered...

That also showed up in my recent visit to the dentist, as it happens. I woke with a full blown migraine, too late to cancel appointments without incurring a cancellation fee. So, skipping breakfast (can't take pills without food) so when the hygienist asked how I was, I told her, full on migraine, thanks. "Sorry to hear that," she muttered, leaving Isle of Wight Radio playing. (not recommended even when you don't have a migraine...) get downstairs to the dentist himself, who checked the teeth, asked the same question, got the same answer. "Turn the noise down, please," he said to the dental nurse, gesturing at his radio. That's consideration. It doesn't happen very often, but when it does, it's good.

It could make a lot of difference to the way your character reacts in any given situation. I had a very bad birth experience. I never had another child because of it. Such things colour a life. So ... how does sickness/accident/wounds/whatever and the way it is treated affect the life of your character(s)?

And how does he cope with visits to the dentist?

Dreams

We all have them. If you didn't have a dream you wouldn't be reading this. Your dream is very likely to see your name on the cover of a pyramid of books in the local store with you signing copies and then emailing friends to say Hollywood has put a bid in for the storyline… am I getting close?

Remember everyone has a secret dream. Something to think about when building a character for a book but even a short story can benefit from a dream hidden deep inside someone.

Dealing with death

We all handle bereavement in different ways. A lot depends on your faith or beliefs, which need to be taken into account when dealing with death in your novel or story. That's why I mentioned religion earlier in this character section. It's important that you think about it, how it affects different people, as that gives a massive insight into their psyche, which is at the basis of all characterisation.

And how they handle a funeral. Do they visit the funeral parlour to view their loved one every day up to the funeral itself? And there is the choice of resting place, burial in a churchyard, burial in a woodland cemetery with just a tree as your memorial, or cremation and someone left to get rid of your ashes, according to the expressed wishes or not, depending on whether a will was left and intentions made clear before the character managed to pass over.

And afterwards, the nastiness afterwards is a good source of material for stories, recriminations over who had what in the way of heirlooms, who 'stole' the best items (even if they were willed to that person) how the money (if there was any) had been divided up… oh I have a hundred stories about funerals, but I know you will have too. Go dig them out. They're there to be mined. Like all the other memories you're storing which are riches indeed for a writer.

~*~*~

Finally...

Before we go into a different aspect of writing, think on this one question in relation to your hero: does he tell the truth?

Part Three

Background – that vital ingredient

Everything affects everyone at some time in some way.

Whatever the Weather

Three crows flew low over the fresh mound in the Linden burying-ground, dark as the thoughts of the three unmourning mourners. These were the widow, Amelia Linden, and the two tall sons, Benjamin and Asahel. The funeral assembly had gone. The clomp of horses' feet and the rattle of wheels were faint down the frozen lane. Then a wind keened far off in the west, nosed across the hills and leaped into the clearing, snapping its fangs at the limbs of the oak trees. The last leaves shivered to earth and scurried like thin brown rats across the grave.

The Sojourner, Marjorie Kinnan Rawlings

Apart from being an object lesson on how to open a book, with death and drama, Ms Rawlings has cleverly used weather as her background to this most startling beginning.

We aren't told simply that the lane is frozen, but that the 'clomp of horses' feet and the rattle of wheels were faint down the frozen lane'. This is very much 'Show Not Tell' writing. The metaphor for cold is continued as 'the last leaves shivered to earth'.

Weather is the favourite topic of conversation for the British; ever changing, never predictable. Sport is affected by it with waterlogged, frozen or snowbound courses or pitches. In summer, festivals, carnivals and fetes are affected by it, too.

Weather is often overlooked by writers.

Consider...

Romance: a moonlit night can become overcast, with rain dampening the ardour of the moment; causing the elegant gown of the heroine to become soggy and mud splattered, not to mention its effect on hairstyle and makeup...

Crime: how much better to commit murder under the heavy disguise of thick fog, or sea fog rolling in to obscure the view from any passer-by.

Horror: what would horror writers do without dark nights, ragged cloud, full moons and howling gales? On the other hand, how much more startling can horror be in a bright summer setting?

But it goes further than contemporary writing. Weather can affect the way you look at any aspect of history. Did you know, for example, that from 1090 onwards the weather was more or less consistently wet for many years? In that year, a severe storm caused flooding which damaged London Bridge; in 1091 several excessively severe storms occurred in autumn, 'with churches struck by lightning. Salisbury Cathedral's spire was thrown down. That year London Bridge was actually swept away by the floods. This weather lasted until 1100. What a difference that kind of detail makes to a story.

What could you conjure up by knowing that the Thames was frozen over on Old Christmas Day in 1142 (before the change to the Gregorian calendar) Truly a Victorian Christmas card scene must have taken place in real life: skaters, chestnut sellers and children, all on the ice. Then again, in 1138 the Thames dried up and could be crossed on foot.

Closer to today, the rains of July 1828 were exceptionally violent, causing considerable flooding. Hay was washed away by the weather and cornfields laid flat. It was a very bad year for sheep rot.

During my research for a historical novel, I discovered that between June and November 1799 there were only eight dry days. (What price global warming?) The harvest was lost in its entirety and there were food shortages in England. I then discovered, from the Archives of the Met Office, that the winter of 1800 was wet and mild. I had to change a good deal of the opening of my ongoing novel set at that time. I assumed it had been sharp and cold but logically, if there had been that much wet weather about, it would have continued - and it did. Those of us in the UK will not forget the freezing endless winter of 1963 or the hurricane of 1987.

Where then do you find this invaluable information? Much of mine comes from a long out-of-print book called Agricultural Records, AD 220-1977 by JM Stratton, bought through a book search company. Attention to detail in historical writing makes all the difference; even if your reader doesn't know what the weather was like at that time to know if you are accurate or not, knowing you are gives you a good foundation on which to build the story.

The Sojourner is a farming book, so weather features heavily throughout the story. Asahel's beloved daughter Dolly dies in a snowstorm, the family fortunes are written in the cold winds .and welcome snow, as much as the spring rains and the summer sunshine. Toward the end of the book. Ms Rawlings again uses weather to build atmosphere, as Asahel nears the end of his search for his long-lost brother.

'The Pacific fog was rolling in. Red beacon lights appeared above the piers. In a moment they too were obscured by a tumbling grey mass that must, he thought, resemble ocean breakers. He heard a sound like the bellowing of a bull, another answered, and another, and these, he knew, could only be the fog-horns. Thin high tootings of tugboats sounded in a panic, like mice under the feet of the bulls.'

Yes, weather would play a leading role in a book about farming, but the story was enhanced by the clever use of weather terms. Here the strange sounds are related to what he knows; fog horns sound like bulls, tugboats like mice. It adds to the character even as we near the end of the book, we are seeing the world from a farmer's perspective.

Weather can add so much to a book, it means people do not walk and talk in a vacuum, they do get wet, or over-hot, they do shiver or sweat and that in turn affects what they do. One of Ray Bradbury's stories concerns the actions of people when the heat reaches 95 degrees. Then there is The October Country, also by Ray Bradbury, not just a month, but a time, a place, a season of colours, cold, and evocative smells of fallen rotting leaves.

Don't overlook the weather. It can add so much atmosphere to your writing. I began a story with rain sleeting across a garage forecourt and the gale taking out the electric, sending the hero home to - well, you need to read it!

Colour Me –

'The woman flamed down the road like a macaw.'
Howard Spring, 'Shabby Tiger.'

Using colour in your story or book can bring it to life. That line from Shabby Tiger is the opening sentence: Howard Spring said he wrote it and then had to follow through: she was obviously colourful and obviously going somewhere...

We live in a world of colour. This was brought home vividly; forgive the pun, when my daughter and I watched a DVD of Royal Weddings. We commented that the colour film of the crowds outside Buckingham Palace at the time of the wedding of Queen Elizabeth and Prince Philip showed that virtually everyone was wearing drab colours. That's something to remember if you are setting a book at that time. The war had left us short of material but in any event, as one elderly lady commented, no one seemed interested in brightly coloured coats and hats then. It was much later when everyone was walking around wearing vivid colours.

So, whilst playing Colour Me with your characters' clothes, remember the time and place of your story. Make sure you don't go overboard with bright hues if it was a time of austerity, for example.

But... nature has always been colourful; don't ignore trees in bloom, trees in leaf, trees shedding gold and brown, all the colours of the seasons blending to give us a portrait of beauty all the year round. It is easily overlooked. I photographed a carving outside a church of St George killing the dragon and totally overlooked the daffodils growing at the foot of the sculpture. When I sent the photograph to the Royal Society of St George, the editor commented she would hold it for the next Spring cover 'because of the daffodils.' (She did, it looked great!)

Colour in hair, eyes, skin, surroundings, colour of cars, of curtains, the blaze of neon lights and shop windows which illuminate our high streets at night these days, the colour of our internal organs…

Don't, whatever you do, overlook colour. Even in the drabbest of times, there was something to lighten the day.

Politics

Touchy subject for some, but essential to add into the mix of a novel. The way people vote shows their prejudices and bias and is extremely revealing. The shenanigans of those in high office often reflect on the population too, some decisions are incredibly far reaching and so affect your everyday people.

Your local authority is also a source of politics. Then there is the European Union… there are many ways of getting politics into a story and many ways your characters would reveal their political inclinations. Just selling a TV stand to someone in the week resulted in a discussion on immigration, how to vote in the European elections this coming Thursday, what he would do were he in government… we all do it. It's there. Use it.

Transport

Let's not go too mad here, but:
Horses, carts, donkeys, pony traps, landaus, carriages, cars, lorries, vans, buses, trams, motorbikes, trains, helicopters, planes, ships, yachts, boats, scooters, skateboards, roller blades…

Country

Wherever you place your novel, you need to be sure to bring a sense of the country into it somehow, some way. R F Delderfield's wonderful novels invoke the true English countryside with all its ever changing beauty and ongoing threats due to builders. (Nothing has changed.) Stephen King's huge far ranging books tend to be set in Maine, which he obviously loves and describes in vivid detail around the actions, feelings and thoughts of his characters. For people like me who have never been to the USA, there is a great sense of the land in which the stories take place, much vaster than here, where everything is confined by the coastline, either of the United Kingdom or the island where I live. It made my zombie novel more of a challenge in many ways but, if you as a writer are not challenged, you aren't going to make the supreme effort to be a first class storyteller for your readers.

Australia's hugeness cannot be easily depicted in a novel but Nevil Shute did it time and again.

Lee Child uses the whole of the USA for his character Reacher, again bringing it all vividly alive through a few words here and there.

There are so many examples! It can be done. You just need to think about it and work at it.

Seems I've said that before...

Now you have the basics...

What are your writing dreams? Are you like so many newbies who join writing forums and announce 'I want to give up my day job and write.'? If so, come into the real world, friend: it isn't that easy and it isn't that easy-peasy do-able, either. It can be done, eventually, and it is do-able, if you are prepared to devote a considerable amount of time to it. But none of it will come easy and it definitely wouldn't be a good idea to give up the day job until you make it big and score a three book deal with a traditional publisher.

Or, self-publish on Amazon and join the big time winners, earning enough to buy a house.

It really isn't like that. It's rare for anyone to score a three book deal with anyone unless the company sees a load of $$$/£££ signs hanging over the work that makes them drop everything to get it. Mostly they'll say you need to go through an agent. The agents will say, we're full, no more room on our list, not looking for new clients at this time…

The ones who score big time on Amazon have usually had the work professionally edited and proofed, have invested in cover design and learned the formatting. Then they set about marketing the thing endlessly on every social network there is and then some, driving a load of people completely over the edge by doing it, people who are sick of others promoting their books. The last report was that Amazon had something like 10,000 books A WEEK being uploaded to Kindle. What chance of your probably unedited, not vetted, revised, proofed and worked on book being noticed? And if you did all those things, what chance of it being noticed?

Let's start with basics. To earn a living you need X amount of $ or £. How are you going to get them? It can take a year, two years, even five years to write a book, with no guarantee it will be published at the end of that time. If you are fortunate enough to have it accepted it will be another eighteen months or so before it reaches the shops and a further six months after that before you get your first royalty cheque, minus the advance you had on signing the contract. Meantime you need to eat, drink, be warm, have a roof over your head, pay for your electricity, gas, telephone, car... need I go on?

So you think instead, I'll freelance. Good idea. Write a saleable article, get it in the post, write another, get it in the post and keep this up for the rest of your working life. Most of those articles will come straight back and you will need to revise, polish and find a new market for them, in the hope that the second time out it won't come back. I see lean times ahead...

Is fiction easier, you ask? No. The short story market is declining by the week. No chance for you to get into that field unless you are outstandingly good and even then the magazines which are still taking stories are swamped with good stories they can use, so your chances are slim. One women's magazine now only takes stories from people who have already had stories accepted. Yes, chicken/egg does spring to mind...

Now do you see the logistics of this writing life? It doesn't add up very well. Those who make a full time living out of writing are usually freelancers who have found their niche market and have editors who actually commission work from them or those who have made a real hit with their books and have an ongoing series which builds and builds. You know the big names, you've seen them and how they are promoted by their publishers.

The novelist Howard Spring said in his autobiography, 'when you sell your first book, don't give up your day job.' I would add to that, don't give up your day job until you have a good many sales to your credit and regular money coming in.

Disheartened? Where's your determination? Novelists persevere against all the odds. The author of 'The Thorn Birds' wrote her book in a year, by disciplining herself and writing every single night. Howard Spring held down a full time job at the Manchester Guardian and wrote every evening from seven to ten. He continued that writing practice when he was able to give up the day job, too. You can hold down a day job and be a writer, thousands do. It means dedication, though, no excuses not to write tonight, tomorrow or even the night after that. You make a commitment to your craft and you follow it through.

Then, I am sorry to say, we come to the real heart of writing. Doing it. Putting the words on the screen or the paper or the notebook or however you find it best to work. One forum I used to visit had the 'how do you write, notebook or computer?' question regularly and every time the answers varied tremendously. It depends on what feels best to you. I don't use a notebook, never have. Everything is done straight to computer where it can be instantly revised, or better still, deleted if it's rubbish. Handwritten it's far more difficult to throw away; you might believe you have something priceless and want to hold on to it. If you don't use it, it's of no value and is best thrown away. Then you can start over again with something better.

So, you've done your research, read copies of the magazine(s), know what the average age and income level of the readers is likely to be (you get that from studying the advertisements), you have the submission guidelines, you have the idea, you write your story or article to the correct word length and gone over it and made it right. Please don't get carried away with the idea that another five hundred words won't hurt. They will, it will get you rejected because the magazine editor knows precisely how many words it takes to fill a page or two pages. They don't need the additional words, they don't want the article to spill onto a third page when it is scheduled to fill just two. Be professional. Get the word count right. If you find it hard to prune it down, you need some experience in that. Find a weekly or monthly challenge which requires you to write a story within a set word count – and do it. It is surprising how good you can get after a while.

When your story or article is done, put it away. Archive it for a week or a month. Get busy with something else, the next story; the next article. Don't give it a passing thought. Then, in an idle moment, retrieve it and read it through. The errors, the overwriting, the clichés, the purple prose, will leap out at you (or it should, if you know your craft well enough) and you can ruthlessly prune it back to the pure gold that is the heart of what you had put down as your deathless prose. You begin to see it wasn't quite that deathless and breathless after all, that there were gaping great holes in the storyline or erroneous facts in your article...

When writing anything, remember this: your first reader is not some nameless faceless person out in the street, but an editor. That person has seen it all before and is bored with all that passes over their desk. They are looking for new, fresh, vital, exciting work. They want interesting articles. They are looking for storylines in both stories and novels that shake them up, that make them want to take it home and read properly, characters that jump off the page and stay in the mind, settings so vivid they are almost there. When you can do that, you will sell your work. Before then, there is a long way to go.

It's called revision. It's called editing. It's called all sorts of fancy things but what it comes down to is this: plain hard work. Disheartening work at times, when all you have so carefully put together is pulled apart. It's harder when it's a full length novel but, if the action doesn't follow a sensible pattern, as in action/downtime/action/downtime to keep your reader interested and if the story doesn't hold up to all sorts of minute scrutiny and if you haven't grabbed your reader by the throat from the first line... forget sending it out. Sounds harsh? With upwards of one hundred MS *a week minimum* arriving at most publishers/agents' offices, all they can do is give it a preliminary look and see if it grabs their attention.

And, if you watch people in bookshops – and you should – you'll see they take the book down, read the blurb, open it at the first page, read the first line or chapter and then either put it back or take it to the cash point and buy it.

So, does your first line attract attention? And if it does, will the story carry on from there? So many questions, I know, but if you don't consider them in advance, you'll waste a good deal of time and effort and gain a good deal of disappointment.

I've moved from articles to books but – stories and articles need to meet the same criteria. Good opening hook, solid middle, satisfying ending and a good, interesting if not eye-catching title to go with it. People flick through magazines, you need to stop them in their tracks and get them to read your article. Editors tend to flick through submissions and if they aren't interested or involved from the start, it's rejected.

The real magical secret of good writing, exciting writing is this: only write about what excites and interests you. If it's a novel in your head, make sure you know it completely, the people, the setting, the plot line. Does it excite you, does it make you want to get to the computer and write; does it draw your thoughts during the day? Are you anxious to get back to it? Then you might have something worthwhile. You need to be fired by your idea to make it work.

Read. Read everything and anything. Don't go anywhere without a book close by, read and read and study what you read, how did the author grab your attention, how did they draw you in to the story, how did they hold your attention, what detail was given which built the characters to the point when you could believe in them? Read critically, look for plot flaws and character flaws – you will find them, most published books have errors because not all editors are as good at their job as they should be – and know that you need to avoid making the same mistakes.

Having said all that and given you a hundred reasons to give it up now and go get a job sweeping a store, it has to be said that there is no other profession like it. Artists and musicians get their kicks making beautiful paintings and music. Writers get to create something better – people who come off the page and into our lives, who become part of our culture, part of our way of life. So many characters, from Frodo Baggins through to Harry Potter are part of our life now. The challenge is there, you can do the same thing, if you work at it, dream of it, be dedicated enough to carry it through to the end – writing a blockbuster book is no easy thing, even though many think it is! – and are persistent enough to find a publisher to take it on.

Advice: Drop the dream for now and think with your head instead. Dreams are good, but dreams don't put bread on the table. Or anywhere else, for that matter. If writing is to be more than a hobby to you, or even just a profitable hobby, you need to stop dreaming and start revising and writing. OK?

Writing 'For Love' – is it worth it?

There is an ongoing, almost permanent debate over non-paying and paying markets on any writers' forum, with passionately held views on both sides. Some maintain that anthologies which do not pay are only bought by the contributors, others maintain that the publisher, no matter how small, should send out copies to all contributors as payment, disregarding the fact that if the publisher is small, to send out 20-30 copies would probably bankrupt them...

All that aside, what does it do for you, the author, to be featured in a non paying anthology, newspaper or magazine?

First, you get exposure and begin to build a writing CV. Unless you have managed to be a shining star from the very beginning and sold your first item to a high paying source, you need publication credentials. Showing a CV of accepted material, which goes in print, not on line, is a good way of showing another editor that you have the ability to write.

Second, you don't know who's going to read your story. Impress them enough and they will go looking for more of your work. That is what you need, an audience, a build-up of people who actively look for your stories.

Third, you retain all rights to the stories and can send them out again and again to fee-paying magazines with the possibility of being accepted and paid for the work.

I'm biased - to some degree. I used to edit for Static Movement, a small independent publisher based in Georgia which specialized in dark/horror/fantasy anthologies. The anthologies I had out there have been posted on my Amazon author profile, along with the 20+ anthologies I appear in as well. I have since added my later work, of course, but that was the nucleus of my work at the time.

I know that these anthologies are in US libraries. I also knew they are being bought; one of mine was photographed by a contributor who spotted it on the dashboard of a London bus…

I don't mind giving my work away. Subsequently I gathered all my published stories together in one anthology currently offered online through fiction4all.com. Nothing is wasted.

But we're not done yet. There's a way to go before we get to Babylon with our candles; we need to push on, darkness approaches…

Part Four

From an editor's viewpoint

An editor's life

Most editors work full time at their job, so if I turn back the clock one year, I can for the moment write as if I still edited for a living, rather than editing as an evening job around The Old Curiosity Shop. Thanks to Amazon and other influences, like ever rising costs and the Royal Mail's perpetual hefty increases... the company I was running had to close. But, I had twenty years of experience of editing, as every book we put out needed attention, especially the 'self published' ones.

An editor's life is one of words, words and then more words. Of reaching for the invaluable Hart's Rules or Collins Grammar to make sure what I thought was right was right, if you see what I mean. Of looking with total despair at some of the writing and wondering what I'm going to do with it.

One author writes his books and sends them to an online e-book company without revision of any kind. It is not something he understands. I go over them, revise them, rewrite them and send them back to the publisher. Because, if I return a book to him, edited, revised and rewritten, he cannot see what has been changed. He said so. His exact comment was; I can't see what you've changed. It is as if he is blind to the words he has written and the necessity to get it right. I work with him because he has good ideas and his books sell (when I've rewritten them!) but we have had classic errors such as:

He removed his hands and put them in his pockets.

They were visiting a temple that the driver found in the back of his coach.

One author sent me a book of some twenty six chapters entirely devoted to oral sex. I was bored by page three and sent it back. He sighed and said 'you missed out on reading the longest love letter in history.' I can but hope the person he wrote it for had pleasure in reading it. I didn't.

My favourite 'how not to submit a story' is this:

I live on the Isle of Wight, a small island off the south coast of England, opposite Portsmouth. The small publishing company I was with did not advertise very much as we had a built in mailing list. So imagine the surprise when we received a MS, five pages, a handwritten, badly illustrated story about a dragon which went on holiday to the Isle of Wight. The letter which accompanied it said as we were publishers on the Isle of Wight would we like to put the story out. It had been written by and with the collaboration of a writers' group...

Stories abound of MS which are held together with ribbon, wool, string and other devices, of people who 'booby-trap' their books by inserting something say 48 pages in to find out if the editor has read that far, who put gaudy colours over everything to attract attention, in fact do every single thing possible to put the editor off.

Let me ask you this; if you're bored when reading a paperback, do you finish it, or do you throw it out or give it to a charity shop? If the latter, why should you think an editor will read a book to the end when they are bored out of their skull or know from page one that it will not sell, even if they threw half a million pounds' worth of promotion at it?

Yes, we can tell from page one if it's worth continuing to read. I have been known to get as far as page four and that is really something...

Having said that, today I got to page 6 of 11 and realised I was reading the story by rote, wondering if it was going anywhere, wondering what was going on and did I care – at which point I had to say 'sorry, but no thanks.' I take the view if I'm losing interest then it's very likely the reader will too. If I can't work out what's going on, the reader won't work if out either. That won't bode well for your reputation in the future.

We found, when we were running the publishing house, that if our customers didn't like someone's book, they never said so. What happened was, we would publish a second book by that author and half a dozen people would buy it. The rest would sit there and we would have to remainder it off to some company or other. I have this in mind when I think a story is not up to standard. I imagine the reader getting bored, flipping over the pages, looking for the next one, remembering the name of the person they didn't like and possibly avoiding any future anthologies with that person's work in it. You see how it could work? If I've already said this, forgive me. I am 54 pages into this book now, been back and forward over it that many times I almost wore out the scroll button and still I miss things... but it is important. If you decide to move on and write a novel, remember that name goes with you. Your reputation is at stake. If someone says no thanks, take note, work on it, bring it up to standard, give them only the best and then the best goes with you into the Big Publishing World.

The editor's life is one of endless reading. We eat, drink, sleep and dream reading. Words. Lines. That black on white thing that we take for granted until we have to work on it, dissect it, correct it; sort it.

It does one other thing too, it spoils ordinary reading. I am ultra aware of the mistakes, slips of logic, bad grammar, wrong words in the wrong place. I start criticising the writing and my daughter says: 'you're a mean editor, you are, you're mean!' Maybe I am. I just like things – right.

Work. Rewriting where necessary, sorting tenses, punctuation, looking for wrong words in the wrong place (the favourites are site for sight, reign for rein, confusion over they're, their and there, taught for taut, straight-jacket for strait-jacket, breath for breathe and vice versa – for some reason) and generally searching for things which didn't make sense. Nothing has changed, I still find the same basic mistakes, except that now 'went' for 'gone'; has become the new mistake on the block.

Then I had the luxury of working in a quiet often solitary office, concentrating on the work.

Now it's different because there is nothing so constant as change. Life throws us curveballs, circumstances alter. For a long time it was open the emails, either in the morning at the shop when all was quiet, or evening when all was quiet and I could access the anthology post-box, keen to see who had sent something in.

I used to edit as I read. If the first bit was fine, I go SAVE and carry on reading. If I didn't think it's going any place, come out, write sad rejection email, find the next one. If I get to carry on reading, by the time I reach the end the story is ready to be saved to a flash drive ready to go home and be dropped into the appropriate anthology. It was the only way I could cope with the volume of work, twelve open anthologies at any given time, plus other outside work as well. That wasn't counting my personal writing, that 'outside' work was editing other anthologies for other people, friends I've made through working with them and which is done for nothing. As was the work on the Thirteen Press anthologies.

It's called 'giving something back.' When I began writing, there was no internet, no decent writer's group locally, no help at home, no support from family. It was me and the typewriter and hours of research, writing and rewriting. Rejections were a taunt to keep me going. No one was going to stop me. So, I learned the hard way, write, get rejected, alter, amend, resubmit, sell, move on…

For a long time my aim was to give something back to all who were following the path to Babylon. The internet helped me to stay in touch. I have been involved in a couple of good dedicated online groups, one foundered when the owners tried to change it and it all fell apart (always a dangerous thing to do, meddle with something that works) and the other just got rather silly. If you ask for comments then argue about them when you get them, you're not ready to accept criticism and possibly not ready to go out into the Big World. I dropped that one.

> *Babylon is on the horizon. Let's hurry our footsteps…*

***

Don't upset your editor.

You have refined, revised, polished and even re-polished your article/story/novel and are ready to send it out into the world.

Hold on, there is something you need to do first. Write the cover letter.

Many editors – I am one of them – judge a book by its cover letter. If it's well phrased, succinct and readable, as in good size font and no fancy colours, etc. then the chances are very high that the MS accompanying it will be the same.

The cover letter says everything. A would-be author sent me a book on a CD. The covering letter was typed entirely in capital letters, was pretty much illiterate in its spelling and grammar and told me that the book was 90,000 words (we ask for 40,000) as he got carried away. I did a quick check and yes, the entire book on the CD was in capital letters...

As a small sideline, I sent a query letter/covering letter to an educational publisher with my first MS for their attention. The book was accepted. Later, when I met the editor, she said it was the covering letter which had attracted them more than the MS itself, as it showed I could write. Remember that. I went on to write another nineteen books for the educational reading scheme they had running at the time.

First point then, work on your covering letter. It needs to be professional, clear and precise, as in 'the MS attached is a work of fiction entitled Going To The Movies With A Panda and is 80,000 words in length. I hope you enjoy reading it. My writing credentials are...' and nothing else apart from the requisite SAE if sending by post. Only add something if you're bold enough or confident enough. I don't remember what was in my cover letter but it must have mentioned stealing ideas from my seven year old and twisting them into tales to teach. Hey, that's a good phrase, wish I'd thought of it back then...

The other thing you really must not do is send your work out without revising it. I've mentioned that dreaded word before, several times, but it is vital. Absolutely vital. Revision means going over it and looking for the glaring errors.

It also means polishing. If you put a story or book away for two weeks, longer if you can, when you read it again you will see all the places where you can word it better, or chop words out to make it flow better, or generally tighten it up.

A persistent thought is coming in here.

As an all-out fan of the King, I have loads of CDs of his music. Some are studio tapes of recording sessions rather than the finished product. On one, Elvis is working with a song called 'I'm Leaving.' He goes through it without faltering, gets to the end, says 'man, that's tough.' Then he calls out to the recording engineer (I'm guessing) 'That thing's worth working with.' It sounds fine to me. The finished product, which is remarkably close to the first studio take, is on another CD and you can only just tell that it's been worked on. He revised it, in writing terms. His song 'In The Ghetto' was recorded thirty two times before he achieved the version he was truly happy with it. It's commonplace to see the tracks on the CDs marked 'take 9', for example.

Revision. The polishing, the smoothing, the correcting and more than anything, the getting it totally right before it goes out and makes you look like an idiot when it arrives on someone's desk/computer/whatever.

The other ongoing mistake which I hate is dangling participles or hanging sentences. I've already mentioned these but it's worth saying it again.

The line which got one book rejected, one too many in a book riddled with them, was:

Racing into the hall, he skidded to a stop.

Why not 'He raced into the hall and skidded to a stop.' ???

Watch what you're writing. People rarely do two things at once, as in take off a coat and switch on a light, pour a drink and start cooking *all at the same time*. If you look for them, you will find them in every book you come across, because the editor has either not bothered or missed them entirely. Not me; this editor edits them out ruthlessly.

So, what do editors want?

Sparkling prose, unusual innovative ideas, a complete lack of purple prose, (no stars sprinkled on black velvet and stuff like that. Be different, be cliché-less, be original.

A first class story (or article idea) with no research errors. They are there, look for them... a queen visiting or hearing about a palace that was built one hundred years after her death is just one...

All this set out properly, A4 pages, double spaced if sent by post, single spaced if sent by email (unless the submission guidelines indicate otherwise) as there is nothing worse than endless scrolling to get down the page. For print, put a simple header:

Editor/Davies/page number

And not much else. Some people apparently advocate name, address email and telephone numbers on every page, or so I am told. Check the guidelines. Mostly, though, editors like an uncluttered page to read. I find headers a distraction, because I tend to edit as I read, rather than read and then edit. Why do the job twice when you can do it once? When edited, I lifted the entire MS (if I accepted it) and put it into book form. I didn't need the headers and footers and fancy bits. They would be in the wrong place in the anthology, obviously.

This night I heard about an editor who reads every story three times.

My question was – and is –why? The reader won't give the story three chances. The reader will start reading; if they're bored, the pages will be flipped over and they will move on to the next one. You, the writer, get one chance with 99% of editors.

There aren't many who will devote the time to three reads. My standard response was 'You get one chance with me. If it doesn't feel right, if there's too much bad language (which will make it stick out like a sore thumb from the other stories, not a good idea) if it's dull, if it's overloaded with information we can do without or writing we can do without (back to the revision and cutting of unnecessary words again) it doesn't get a look in.'

What don't editors want... (What I didn't want must surely go for many others, too.) They don't want stories for themed anthologies which had no reference, no bearing on the theme. I once had a story sent in for a Halloween anthology that was not set in, or mentioned, Halloween.

They don't want stories which are as much as 1500 words over the word limit. There is a reason for word limits; it gives more room for other authors to get their work included. You may be wonderful, but not everyone will like you. Make room for the ones they will like.

They don't want stories with totally confused tenses. If you start with third person past, stay there. If you start with third person present, stay there. If you don't know what I mean, or can't see that you're mixing them up, then go get a good book on grammar. It's your job to sort the tenses, not the editor's.

On which subject... a story came in riddled with typos, tenses and punctuation errors. There were no paragraphs. I sent it back and asked for it to be sorted out properly. The comment came back instantly that they considered it was the editor's job to do that, the writer just wrote.

Well, it wasn't this editor's job and I knew no editor who would accept work like that.

On the critique site someone kept posting their snippets of stories as if it was blank verse. Several times they were asked if it was poetry; if so please post in the poetry section. No, they said, it's the way I write. ??? To me that says the person does not read. If you read, you know how print looks on a page, how the paragraphs are indented, how dialogue is set out, how scene breaks are indicated. If you don't know any of this, you had best start studying published books rather than just reading the words. Everything, every last thing, about a published book needs to be something you know. Then you won't send in stories which have no indents, no quotation marks, no scene breaks and no conventional chapter breaks either.

I remember the story which arrived for an anthology. It was 1500 words over the limit, the start was too slow and the tenses were muddled. I sent it back, with comments.. The story came back, identical it seemed to me, it still registered at 1500 words over the word limit and the tenses were still muddled, for another anthology, in the hope it fitted better there...

I found this to be a favourite trick of writers, sending the story back again for another anthology. If it wasn't wanted first time, it's very unlikely to be wanted the second time. Remember the injunction not to add headers and footers to email submissions? That's for a reason: the editor can't take them out. The only way they can lose them is to highlight each page individually and lift it into a fresh document... an editor need to spend time doing that, for sure… and of course your headers and page numbers are useless in an anthology. KISS. Keep It Simple, Stupid. It works for me.

The next step

So there you are; you've done the work, polished and checked and revised and formatted and sent it out.

What next?

Do something else, write something else; don't brood on what people are thinking of your work. If they like it, you'll hear soon enough. If they don't, it will be back with you in record time.

Then you will need to send it out again...

Which leads me into the next section...

When you get rejected...

As this is a common problem, especially for newbies, I thought it was an essential topic for this handbook.

The finest object lesson for rejection is right there in the King's track: 'Guitar Man'.

If ever there was an object lesson on try, try and try again, that song is it! He packs up his job, takes off with his guitar 'and for the next three weeks went a-hunting those night clubs/looking for a place to play.' But no one wanted to know. So he goes further, gets on an overloaded hobo truck (the song truly is a story in lyrics!) finds nowhere to play, no one wanted to hire a guitar man. So he sleeps in the hobo jungle, walks a thousand miles of track, until he finds a nightclub where a four piece band is jamming. He takes his guitar and he sits in... the success story is that people are invited to go to the club where a five piece band is playing and the leader is the swinging little guitar man.

Because he persevered, he didn't hock the guitar and go back to the car wash, he kept right on trying.

When you know your work is up to standard, keep right on trying. I did; 50+ rejections and I finally hit the right editor at the right time with the right proposal and the series (not just the book) sold.

Rejection hurts. It's personal, it's nasty, it's almost vindictive, it's 'what the hell is wrong with those people that they can't see class staring out at them?' and it's 'I can't do this' as well. But you can.

My first writing efforts came back. My second third and fourth stayed out there. My fifth came back and so on, through 30 years of writing (I remember well when I started and the very first fan-fiction story I ever wrote, too, on a £50 Brother portable typewriter on the kitchen table... ah, those were the days...) it's been a roller coaster ride. Until you hit the Big Time, it is. (I'm still waiting...)

The advice really is, if it comes back, put it away for a month, look at it again, see where you can improve it, if you can't, send it out as it is. If you can, do the rewrite and send it out again AND THEN GET ON WITH THE NEXT AND THE NEXT AND THE NEXT! It is always good to have something else ready to send to the editor who says yes, whether it is a filler or a story or a book. They will want to know there is more. So while you wait, get writing.

My 'rejection' story goes on.

In 2005 I channelled a book from a discarnate spirit about his life in medieval times. In 2006 I tried marketing the book. No one wanted to know. It came back time after time. In despair I fell for a marketing email from Equeryonline – for a fee they send out a mass mailing about your book. (I am not saying this is a bad thing, others may find success this way. It was my book which seemed to give people the problem.)

I had over fifty responses. I spent an entire weekend preparing the individual MSS, some wanted all of it; some wanted one chapter, three chapters and so on. They were all despatched to the UK and the USA. Then came the fun.

Some of the agencies Equeryonline targeted had already turned me down but they still asked to see it. One agent wrote 'YES PLEASE!' and then responded by saying I had to submit through his website. A publisher called me from the States to say they wanted it but their books were 'subsidised' and I had no money.

One asked for the ending to be changed 'because it was too sad' when I had clearly stated the book was based on a real life. In real life he was executed. Famously. How could I change that?

Another agent said, 'historical fiction is hot right now, let me see it,' and then responded with 'I don't do historical fiction.' Someone else told me they only took fiction – to which I responded that the 'autobiography' of someone who died in 1478 could be classed as fiction, could it not? No answer.

The agencies that had seen it before turned it down again. In the end every last one rejected it.

Then, talking to an editor who had published my work in the past, I discovered that his company were looking to sideline into historical work, travel, crime and thrillers. I told him of my book, he asked to see it and took it twenty four hours later. 'Death Be Pardoner To Me', the life of George, duke of Clarence, is on sale right now through fiction4all.com. The follow up books were written, Judas Iskariot, Henry VIII, Guy Fawkes, Charles I, Jacquetta Woodville, all available from the same publisher. (I am a medium who works directly with spirit authors, these are their books, their stories, their lives, unadorned and adulterated by historians. Believe or not believe; the books are good reads either way.)

There are two lessons from this.

One is; believe in what you do. If I had not believed in the book I would not have mentioned it to the editor and then got it into print.

The other is; sheer luck comes into it at times. Remember how JK Rowling got the publishers interested? Someone took the MS home; their daughter read it and wanted to know more. An American author self-published a book, an agent bought it; read it and took him on.

My favourite rejection story of all time is the publisher who wrote:

Mr Kipling, you do not understand how to use the English language.

Then there's the nineteen publishers who turned down The Day Of The Jackal as 'everyone knew the ending.'…

Success, and it came to both Rudyard Kipling and Frederick Forsythe, along with the others, their Babylon if you like, came about through having a Good Product to offer or for someone to find. It has to be right. Many self published e-books are not really good enough for anything but being an ego e-book for the author, it's sad to say. I've read enough of them to say they aren't worth the effort or the money. Some are good, no question of it, but lack that edge, that tiny bit extra which makes them Good Enough. To get recognised and accepted, it has to be Good Enough. We are back to the revision/edit/revision thing again. My first historical book was good enough to be instantly accepted by my editor and for him to say he was 'blown away' by it, and my subsequent books, too.

We cannot avoid rejection. It is part of the writing life and you need to grow a thick skin so as not to be hurt by it. So many people see it as a personal insult; they write nasty letters back, they call people names. I had the opportunity of attending a literary agents' version of Dragon's Den. After Round 2 ten names were called. One lady, who really thought she had made it through, stomped out, muttering 'bastards!' I didn't make it, but I did place the book.

Rejection means that person didn't like that work at that time. Rejection means possibly you have to tone down or alter or amend your style if you want to get into that particular magazine or anthology. If it isn't that important to you and you can find someone else to take it, go right ahead. As long as you get accepted somewhere… the rejection should not matter. But it does, it still hurts. I've sent what I consider top class stories to anthologies, been shortlisted and then lost out. The story I wrote on that day trip, the one which was triggered by my bread, was shortlisted for an anthology in Australia, after it had appeared in two separate SF magazines. I would have liked that acceptance but it was not to be. (It's a bit sugary; it won't find a place in my anthologies…) Another which I wrote for After Death almost made it. Almost. That sad word, along with if. The anthology won an award with the Horror Writers' Association. That editor knew precisely what he wanted to make a first class anthology. Mine wasn't quite right.

Use your acceptances as the buffer, 'look, someone does like my work' and concentrate on getting a writing CV together. Gain yourself a reputation as a good writer. When the MS goes out, people will remember you.

That way rejection won't be anywhere near so bad.

Remember this: Every editor has their own needs, their own way of working, their own requirements and, most of all, their own opinion. Everything I say when rejecting a story is my opinion. Rejected because it didn't suit me.

This happens all the time. An anthology was created called The Morgue. I wrote a story for it called Danse Macabre. Everyone in the story was dead, so I expressed the dialogue like this:

Dead Lydia staggered across the room, round the dissecting table and got to the cabinets.

I need company! She pulled and tugged and reluctantly the first drawer slid open. The man inside, elderly, lined, haggard and half starved, blinked and looked up at her.

Is it time to get up?
If you want.
I do. It's boring lying here like that. Nothing to look at.
I need the company.

The man sat up and pushed himself off the tray which had been holding him.

That's a good idea. Let's find some more people.

The editor rejected it immediately, saying the title had been used (now there's a surprise and there's no copyright on titles anyway...) and the dialogue was not set out properly.

I said OK, no problem. He resigned and handed the anthology over to someone else. I took a chance, resubmitted and it was accepted.

That's much the same story as my novel rejected by Nexus. I had adversely commented on their first ever Black Lace publication. Then I made the mistake of sending them my newest book. They sent a two page rejection letter - and I sold the book within a week. It has since been in print three times. So much for a knowledgeable editor... actually, seriously, I can say this as the company is dead, they were not knowledgeable at all. The first rule of erotic writing, the serious never-to-be-broken first rule of erotic writing is that *children are not mentioned anywhere at any time.* The book in question then opened with a girl turning up at a house to take a job as governess to two small children.

As with the contrived plot lines, how much thought would it have taken for that foolish author to make the governess into a secretary instead? So the very first Black Lace book went out with that in it. And I had a two page rejection letter, a massive over reaction, because they were wrong and they knew it. Professionals can be as bitchy as any independents; don't expect better treatment from them if you go that course. In fact, the independents have been far more charming, helpful, co-operative and full of guidance than any traditional publisher I have met so far. In 30+ years that's quite a few people.

Back to the point here. ALL editorial decisions are editorial opinions. If I don't see any merit in a story loaded with unnecessary detail, food, travel, conversations, if I find dialogue too formal for its storyline, that's my opinion. Another editor will leap on it and say 'great!'

I wrote my story The Day Death Wore Boots for my anthology Ghost Stories Western Style. Rather than assume it had any merit, I sent it to two editors, one in the UK, one in the USA, asking for their opinions as friends. The US editor said it was dreadful and needed a total rewrite, the UK editor said it was fantastic and she loved it. It went into the anthology and, as I already said, appeared in Science Fiction Trails in 2013. Another short story site said it was the best story I had sent her out of close on fifty. (It has since been the title and lead story in her anthology of ghost stories!)

Sometimes you have to go with your instincts. When you've written enough you'll know what's good and what's indifferent. Sometimes you have to listen to an editor, too. My advice is always this: if the comments strike a chord with you, take notice. If they don't, ignore them. The truth is; I needed a second opinion on that Western story for my peace of mind. It actually came from a surprising source who told me it was good and I really should have accepted that. As it happens… it gave me an anecdote to share with you in this little book.

Three quarters of my stories, maybe more, come from spirit authors these days. If you look at them closely, you can see the differences. The main thing is, they are all superbly written. Not one spirit is a bad author. With their help, I got to Babylon sooner than I hoped. My candle died as I got to the gate and the gatekeeper lit my way in with his lantern.

***

We are at the gates of Babylon now. There's very little else I can tell you, except that you will hear people talk of your developing your own 'voice'. That's shorthand for your own distinctive style of writing. It comes from endless writing, developing itself as you go without you realising it. You can't 'find' it, it happens.

Light your candles, find your quills, pens, fingers, whatever, and get writing. The world needs stories. The earliest of men sat around a fire and listened to the Shaman telling folk tales, which were old back then. (How do I know this? You'll need to read my book set 30,000 years ago to find out, but believe me, they did) and we have needed storytellers ever since. Whether your story has a moral, a theme, a meaning or just pure entertainment, it is needed by someone, somewhere. Stories to think about when the book is put down, stories to think about when sleep won't come. Stories that somehow answer questions you have had and set them at peace. Stories which comfort, surprise, excite, chill and thrill.

If I've gone the tiniest way toward helping you achieve that, this journey to Babylon and the chats we have had along the way will have been more than worthwhile.

See you there.

Information:

Check this out for the fun of seeing what someone else has used for 'he said'… they are really good!
http://badpets.net/Humor/LongLists/TomSwifties.html

Prediction Challenge
http://predictionfiction.blogspot.co.uk/
Every week we get three different words chosen at random, around which we need to weave a 100 word story. Several of us are running serials at the moment. The standards are incredibly high, to win is everything!

Advice from Ray Bradbury
http://www.openculture.com/2012/04/ray_bradbury_gives_12_pieces_of_writing_advice_to_young_authors_2001.html

Forever
Available as a download or paperback from fiction4all.com
as are my historical fiction books.

The Skullface Chronicles is available as a download or paperback through fiction4all.com

www.ingramcontent.com/pod-product-compliance
Lightning Source LLC
Chambersburg PA
CBHW071700040426
42446CB00011B/1845